Tucholsky Wagner Zola Scott Sydow Freud Schlegel
Turgenev Wallace Fonatne
Twain Walther von der Vogelweide Fouqué Friedrich II. von Preußen
Weber Freiligrath Frey
Kant Ernst
Fechner Weiße Rose von Fallersleben Richthofen Frommel
Fichte Hölderlin
Engels Fielding Eichendorff Tacitus Dumas
Fehrs Faber Flaubert
Eliasberg Ebner Eschenbach
Feuerbach Maximilian I. von Habsburg Fock Zweig
Eliot Vergil
Ewald
Goethe London
Elisabeth von Österreich
Mendelssohn Balzac Shakespeare Dostojewski Ganghofer
Lichtenberg Rathenau Doyle Gjellerup
Trackl Stevenson Hambruch
Tolstoi Lenz Droste-Hülshoff
Mommsen Hanrieder
Thoma von Arnim
Dach Verne Hägele Hauff Humboldt
Reuter Rousseau Hagen Hauptmann Gautier
Karrillon Garschin
Defoe Baudelaire
Damaschke Hebbel
Descartes Hegel Kussmaul Herder
Wolfram von Eschenbach Dickens Schopenhauer
Darwin Melville Grimm Jerome Rilke George
Bronner Bebel
Campe Horváth Aristoteles Voltaire Federer Proust
Bismarck Vigny Barlach Herodot
Gengenbach Heine
Storm Casanova Tersteegen Grillparzer Georgy
Chamberlain Lessing Langbein Gilm Gryphius
Brentano Lafontaine
Strachwitz Claudius Schiller Kralik Iffland Sokrates
Katharina II. von Rußland Bellamy Schilling
Gerstäcker Raabe Gibbon Tschechow
Löns Hesse Hoffmann Gogol Wilde Vulpius
Luther Heym Hofmannsthal Klee Hölty Morgenstern Gleim
Roth Heyse Klopstock Kleist Goedicke
Luxemburg Puschkin Homer Mörike
La Roche Horaz Musil
Machiavelli Kierkegaard Kraft Kraus
Navarra Aurel Musset
Nestroy Marie de France Lamprecht Kind Kirchhoff Hugo Moltke
Laotse Ipsen Liebknecht
Nietzsche Nansen
Marx Ringelnatz
von Ossietzky Lassalle Gorki Klett Leibniz
May vom Stein Lawrence Irving
Petalozzi Knigge
Platon Pückler Michelangelo Kock Kafka
Sachs Poe Liebermann
de Sade Praetorius Mistral Zetkin Korolenko

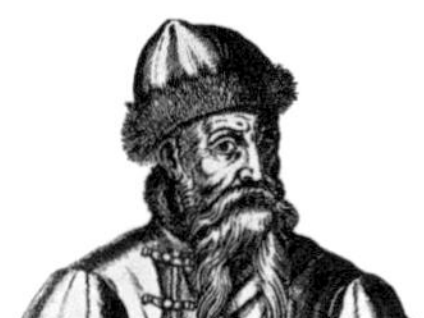

The publishing house tredition has created the series **TREDITION CLASSICS**. It contains classical literature works from over two thousand years. Most of these titles have been out of print and off the bookstore shelves for decades.

The book series is intended to preserve the cultural legacy and to promote the timeless works of classical literature. As a reader of a **TREDITION CLASSICS** book, the reader supports the mission to save many of the amazing works of world literature from oblivion.

The symbol of **TREDITION CLASSICS** is Johannes Gutenberg (1400 – 1468), the inventor of movable type printing.

With the series, tredition intends to make thousands of international literature classics available in printed format again – worldwide.

All books are available at book retailers worldwide in paperback and in hardcover. For more information please visit: www.tredition.com

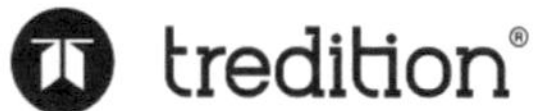

tredition was established in 2006 by Sandra Latusseck and Soenke Schulz. Based in Hamburg, Germany, tredition offers publishing solutions to authors and publishing houses, combined with worldwide distribution of printed and digital book content. tredition is uniquely positioned to enable authors and publishing houses to create books on their own terms and without conventional manufacturing risks.

For more information please visit: www.tredition.com

An Art-Lovers Guide to the Exposition

Sheldon Cheney

Imprint

This book is part of the TREDITION CLASSICS series.

Author: Sheldon Cheney
Cover design: toepferschumann, Berlin (Germany)

Publisher: tredition GmbH, Hamburg (Germany)
ISBN: 978-3-8491-4878-2

www.tredition.com
www.tredition.de

Copyright:
The content of this book is sourced from the public domain.

The intention of the TREDITION CLASSICS series is to make world literature in the public domain available in printed format. Literary enthusiasts and organizations worldwide have scanned and digitally edited the original texts. tredition has subsequently formatted and redesigned the content into a modern reading layout. Therefore, we cannot guarantee the exact reproduction of the original format of a particular historic edition. Please also note that no modifications have been made to the spelling, therefore it may differ from the orthography used today.

Contents

Foreword

This handbook is designed to furnish the information necessary for intelligent appreciation of the purely artistic features of the Exposition. It is planned first to explain the symbolism of the architecture, sculpture and painting; and second, to point out the special qualities that give each artistic unit its individual appeal. It is made for the intelligent observer who, having enjoyed the purely aesthetic impression of the various works of art, feels a legitimate curiosity about their meaning.

Everything possible has been done to make the volume a guide rather than merely a general treatise. The chapter groupings are the most obviously serviceable ones. Running heads will be found at the tops of the pages, and the sub-headings and catch-titles in each chapter are designed to make reference. to individual features as easy as possible. A complete index is added at the end.

Purely destructive criticism and ridicule have been carefully avoided. But if the writer did not pretend to a power of artistic discrimination which is lacking in the average layman who has not specialized in art and architecture, there would be little excuse for preparing the guide. The praise and criticism alike are such, it is hoped, as will aid the less practiced eye to see new beauties or to establish sounder standards of judgment.

Acknowledgment is made to the official Exposition press bureau for courtesies received, and to those artists who have supplied information about their own work. For obvious reasons no material has been accepted direct from articles and books already published. If certain explanations of the symbolism seem familiar, it is only because all wordings of the ideas echo the artists' interpretations as given out by the press bureau.

Acknowledgment is due also to the Cardinell-Vincent Company, official photographers, since most of the illustrations are from their prints.

S. C.

The Architecture and Art as a Whole

In the art of the Exposition the great underlying theme is that of achievement. The Exposition is being held to celebrate the building of the Panama Canal, and to exhibit to the world evidences of the progress of civilization in the decade since the last great exposition- a period among the richest in the history of civilization. So the ideas of victory, achievement, progress and aspiration are expressed again and again: in the architecture with its triumphal arches and aspiring towers; in the sculpture that brings East and West face to face, and that shows youth rising with the morning sun, eager and unafraid; and in the mural paintings that portray the march of civilization, and that tell the story of the latest and greatest of mankind's triumphs over nature. But perhaps the most significant thing of all is the wonderfully harmonious and unified effect of the whole, that testifies so splendidly to the perfect co-operation of American architects, sculptors and painters.

The dominant note artistically is harmony. At no other exposition have the buildings seemed to "hold together" so well; and at no other has there been the same perfect unity of artistic impression. The Chicago Exposition of 1893 focused the artistic expression of the nation at that time. It brought about the first great awakening of the country in artistic matters, and it practically revolutionized American architecture. The St. Louis Exposition of 1904, while less unified in plan, gave another great stimulus to architecture, and especially to sculpture. But the Panama-Pacific Exposition should have a more far-reaching effect than either of these, because its great lesson is not in the field of any one art, but in showing forth the immense value of coordination of all the arts in the achievement of a single glorious ideal. The great thing here is the complete harmony of purpose, of design, and of color, in the combined work of architects, sculptors, painters, and landscape gardeners. The sensible plan that results in perfect convenience in getting about, the clothing of this plan in noble and fitting architectural forms, the use of sculpture and painting as an integral part of the architectural scheme, the tying in of buildings to site with appropriate planting, and the pulling together of the whole composition with harmonious color-these are the things that will leave their impress on American art for all time to come. If each student of the art of the Exposition takes home with him an understanding of the value of this synthesis, of this co-ordination of effort, he will have the key to the Exposition's most valuable heritage to the American people.

Physically there are three distinct parts to the Exposition: the main group of exhibit palaces, the Zone, and the state and foreign buildings. The art-lover will be concerned almost entirely with the first of these; for artistically the Zone expresses anarchy, and the state and foreign pavilions are given over almost entirely to social and commercial interests.

Architecture

The architecture of the central group of palaces and courts is a notable departure from that of most of the expositions of the past. There are none of the over decorated facades, none of the bizarre experiments in radical styles, and little of the riot of extraneous ornament, that have been characteristic of typical "exposition architecture." The whole spirit here is one of seriousness, of dignity, of permanency. The effects are obtained by the use of long unbroken lines, blank wall spaces, perfect proportioning, and a restrained hand in decoration. Color alone is relied upon to add the spirit of gayety without which the architecture might be too somber for its joyous purpose.

The ground plan is remarkable for its perfect symmetry. On the main east and west axis are grouped eight palaces, about three interior courts. At the east end the axis is terminated by the Palace of Machinery, which cuts off the main group from the Zone. On the west the axis is terminated by the Fine Arts Palace, which separates the central group from the state and foreign buildings. The main cross axis is terminated at the south by the Tower of Jewels and the Fountain of Energy, and at the north by the Column of Progress on the Marina. The two minor cross axes end at the south in the Horticulture Palace and Festival Hall-the two great domed structures that naturally would separate themselves from the main plan and at the north these axes open on the Marina and the beautiful bay view.

This plan is admirably compact. It has the effect of a walled city, giving a sense of oneness from without, and a sense of shelter from within. The plan eliminated the usual great distances between exhibit halls, at the same time providing protection against the winds that occasionally sweep over the Exposition area. More important still, the throwing of the finer architectural effects into the inner courts allowed freedom in individual expression. In the court system the architects obtained unity with great variety of style, and harmony without monotony.

The plan was worked out by a commission of architects. But the greatest credit must be given to Edward H. Bennett, who first conceived the walled-city idea, and who brought his long experience in city-planning to serve in determining the best method of utilizing the magnificent site.

The style of architecture cannot be summed up in any one name. Practically every historic style has been drawn upon, but there are very few direct copies from older buildings. The old forms have been used with new freedom, and occasionally with very marked originality. As one looks down on the whole group of buildings, the Oriental feeling dominates, due to the many Byzantine domes. In the courts and facades the Renaissance influence is strongest, usually Italian, occasionally Spanish. Even where the classic Greek and Roman elements are used, there is generally a feeling of Renaissance freedom in the decoration. One court is in a wonderful new sort of Spanish Gothic, perfectly befitting California. In the styles of architecture, as in the symbolism of painting and sculpture and in the exhibits, one feels that the East and West have met, with a new fusion of national ideals and forms.

The material used in the buildings is a composition, partaking of the nature of both plaster and concrete, made in imitation of Travertine, a much-prized building marble of Italy. This composition has the warm ochre tone and porous texture of the original stone, thus avoiding the unpleasant smoothness and glare which characterize stucco, the usual Exposition material.

Sculpture

In one way more than any other, the sculpture here surpasses that of other expositions: it is an integral part of the larger artistic conception. It not only tells its individual stories freely and beautifully, but it fits perfectly into the architectural scheme, adding the decorative touch and the human element without which the architecture would seem bare.

The late Karl Bitter was chief of the department of sculpture, and although there is no single example of his work on the grounds, it was he who, more than any other, insisted upon a close relationship between the architecture and the sculpture. A. Stirling Calder was acting chief, and he had charge of the actual work of enlarging the models of the various groups and placing each one properly.

The material of the sculptures is the same as that of the buildings, Travertine, thus adding to the close relationship of the two.

Mural Paintings

The mural paintings as a whole are not so fine as either the architecture or the sculpture. The reason can be traced perhaps to the fact that painting does not readily bow to architectural limitations. In this case the artists, with the exception of Frank Brangwyn, who painted the canvases for the Court of Abundance, were limited to a palette of five colors, in order that the panels should harmonize with the larger color scheme.

Color

Never before was there an exposition in which color played such a part. Here for the first time a director of color was placed above architect and sculptor and painter. Jules Guerin, chief of color decoration, has said that he went to work just as a painter starts to lay out a great picture, establishing the warm buff of the building walls as a ground tone, and considering each dome or tower or portal as a detail which should add its brilliant or subdued note to the color harmony. Not only do the paintings and sculpture take proper place in the tone scheme, but every bit of planting, every strip of lawn and every bed of flowers or shrubs, has its duty to perform as color accent or foil. Even the gravel of the walks was especially chosen to shade in with the general plan.

As seen from the heights above the Exposition-and no visitor should go away without seeing this view-the grounds have the appearance of a great Oriental rug. The background color is warm buff, with various shades of dull red against it, accented by domes and columns of pale green, with occasional touches of blue and pink to heighten the effect.

In the courts the columns and outer walls are in the buff, or old ivory, tone, while the walls inside the colonnades have a "lining color" of Pompeian red; the ceilings are generally cerulean blue; the cornices are touched with orange, blue and gold; and occasional columns of imitation Siena marble, and bronzed statues, set off the whole.

In connection with the color scheme, great credit must be given to John McLaren, chief of the department of landscape gardening, who has worked so successfully in co-operation with architects and color director. The Exposition is built almost entirely on filled ground, just reclaimed from the bay; and it was a colossal task to set out the hundreds of thousands of flowers, shrubs and trees which now make the gardens seem permanent, and which set off the architecture so perfectly.

Lighting

When one's soul has been drenched all day in the beauty of courts and palaces and statues and paintings, dusk is likely to bring welcome rest; but when the lights begin to appear there comes a new experience-a world made over, and yet quite as beautiful as the old. Walls are lost where least interesting, bits of architecture are brought out in relief against the velvet sky, and sculptures take on a new softness and loveliness of form. Under the wonderfully developed system of indirect illumination, no naked light is seen by the eye; only the soft reflected glow, intense when desired, but never glaring. If this lighting is not in itself an art, it is at least the informing spirit that turns prose to poetry, or the instrumental accompaniment without which the voice of the artist would be but half heard. Too much credit cannot be given to the lighting wizard of the Exposition, W. D'Arcy Ryan.

The Court of Abundance

The Court of Abundance is the most original, and perhaps the most consistently beautiful, of all the Exposition courts. No other is so clearly complete in itself, without the intrusion of features from surrounding buildings and courts. No other has the same effect of cloistered seclusion partly because each of the others is open on one side. And certainly no other indicates so clearly the touch of the artist, of the poet-architect, from the organic structural plan to the finest bit of detail. Even the massive central fountain, though conceived in such different spirit, has no power to dispel the almost ethereal charm that hovers over the place.

The distinctive note of the court is one of exquisite richness. As one enters from any side the impression grows that this is the most decorative of all the courts; and yet one is not conscious of any individual bit of decoration as such. Everything fits perfectly: arches, tower, cornices, finials, statues, planting-it all goes to enrich the one impression. Someone has said that the court is not architecture, but carving; and that suggests perfectly the decorative wealth of the composition.

Architecture

The style of architecture has been guessed at as everything from Romanesque and Gothic to Flamboyant Renaissance and Moorish. The truth is that the court is a thoroughly original conception; and the architect has clothed his pre-conceived design in forms that he has borrowed from all these styles as they happened to suit his artistic purpose. The spirit of the court is clearly Gothic, due to the accentuation of the vertical lines-and one will note how the slender cypresses help the architecture to convey this impression. The rounded arches, modified in feeling by the decorative pendent lanterns, hint of the awakening of the Renaissance period in Spain, during the Fourteenth and Fifteenth Centuries, when the vertical lines, and decorative leaf and other symbolic ornaments of the severer Gothic, were so charmingly combined with classic motives.

The architecture here is inspiring as a symbol of the American "melting-pot." It is a distinct and original evolution, recalling the great arts of Europe, and yet eluding classification. The court shows that the designer was master of the styles of the past, but refused to be a slave to them; at the same time he had an original conception but did not let it run into the blatant and bizarre. It is from such fusions of individual genius with the traditions of the past that a distinctive American architecture is most likely to flower.

The tower is a magnificent bit of architectural design. It is massive and yet delicate. It dominates the court, and yet it fits perfectly into the cloister. The rich sculpture is so much a part of the decorative scheme that there is no impression of the structure having been "ornamented." One must search long in the histories of architecture to find a tower more satisfying.

The architect who designed the Court of Abundance is Louis Christian Mullgardt, one of the two most original geniuses among California's architects.

It is well to enjoy this court at first for its beauty alone, without regard to its rich symbolism. One who has thus considered it, merely as a delight to the eye, usually is surprised to find that it has a deeper underlying meaning than any of the other courts. The present name, "Court of Abundance," is not the original one. The architect conceived it as "The Court of The Ages." It is said that the Exposition directors, for the rather foolish reason that a Court of the Ages would not fit into the scheme of a strictly contemporaneous exposition, re-christened it "The Court of Abundance." But it is the former name that sums up the thought behind the decorative features.

The underlying idea is that of evolution. The tower sculptures, which will be more fully explained in following paragraphs, represent successive ages in the development of man-the Stone Age, the Mediaeval Age, and the Present Age. The decoration of the cloisters may be taken as symbolizing the evolution of primitive man from the lower forms of life. Thus the ornamental garlands that run up the sides of the arches are of seaweed, while other parts of the decoration show crabs, lobsters and other of the lower forms of sea life.

Higher up the ornament includes conventionalized lilies suggestive of higher plant life. And surmounting the colonnade, one over each pier, are the repeated figures of primitive man and primitive woman. It is at this height that the tower sculptures begin, carrying on the story of man up to the present age. At a level between the Stone Age group and the Mediaeval Age is a row of cocks, symbols of the rise of Christianity. Perhaps the whole aspiring feeling of the court is meant to further suggest the upward rise of man-but after all, the purely sensuous beauty of the architecture is sufficient to warrant its being, without any straining after symbolism.

Sculpture

Groups on the Tower. The three main groups typify the rise of man, and especially the rise of man's civilization through religion. The lowest group, over the main arch, is called The Stone Age. Along the base are prehistoric monsters, and above are figures representing various phases of primitive life, as a man strangling an animal with his hands, and a figure that may suggest the rude beginnings of art or industry. The heads indicate a period of evolution when man was not very different from the ape; but the central figures suggest the development of family life, and a new outlook and a seeking for something higher.

The middle group, The Mediaeval Age, shows an armored figure with sword and shield, a crusader perhaps, with the force of religion symbolized in the priest or monk at one side, and the force of arms suggested by the archer at the other, these being the two forces by which man was rising in that age.

The third and highest group represents The Spirit of the Present Age enthroned. At one side a child holds the book of learning, while at the other a child holds the wheel of industry. The group also carries inevitably a suggestion of motherhood.

Flanking the middle group are two figures, in which the whole idea of human evolution is suggested by a modern man and woman outgrowing their old selves. On the east and west faces of the tower are figures representing "Thought."

All the sculpture on the tower is by Chester Beach.

Figures Surmounting Colonnade. Two figures of "The Primitive Man" and one of "The Primitive Woman" are repeated above the cloister all around the court. The woman carries a child on her back, one man is feeding a pelican, and the other is a hunter returning with a club in one hand and his quarry in the other. These figures are remarkably well suited to their purpose, balancing one another exactly; they are so much a part of the decorative scheme, indeed, that the average person is likely to overlook their merits as individual statues. Albert Weinert was the sculptor.

The Water Sprites. At the tower side of the court, flanking the stairway that leads to the archway under the tower, are two free-standing monuments that were designed as fountains. The original plan called for cascades from below the Stone Age group on the tower to these monuments. Although the elimination of this feature made the court more simple and satisfying as a whole, the figures of the Water Sprites were left high and dry, so that now there is a certain incongruity in their position. Still one may admire the very spirited girl archers surmounting the two columns, even if they are apparently launching arrows at their sister sprites below, instead of into jets of water as was intended. The figures at the bases of the columns, while lacking the grace and the joyous verve of those above, still are very decorative. All are the work of Leo Lentelli.

The Fountain of Earth. In the large basin in the center of the Court of Abundance is Robert Aitken's "Fountain of Earth." While plainly out of keeping with the spirit of the court, this is in itself one of the most powerful and most interesting sculptural compositions at the Exposition. It is deeply intellectual, and more than any other group it requires an explanation of the symbolism before one can appreciate it.

The fountain is really in two compositions. The larger, and central, one is composed of a globe representing the earth, with four panels of figures on the four sides, representing certain of the incidents of life on earth, or certain riddles of existence. The secondary composition lies to the south of the central one, on the same pedestal; and this is divided into two groups by a formalized wing through the center. The two scenes here represent life before and after earthly existence. The two huge arms and the wing are all that can be seen of Destiny, the force with which the allegorical story begins and ends.

To "read" the fountain in proper sequence, one must start with the west face of the secondary group. This represents The Beginning of Things. The arm of Destiny is calling forth life and points the way to the earth. The three women figures next to the hand show the gradual awakening from Oblivion. The adjoining two figures represent the kiss of life or of love, and the woman is holding forth to the earth the children created of that love. The entire group on this west face, considered in relation to the main composition, may be taken as representing the peopling of the earth.

There is now a gap which one must pass over, to reach the South panel of the central composition. This gap represents the lost period of time between the peopling of the earth and the beginning of history.

The South panel of the main structure has as its central figure Vanity with her hand-glass. Whether the artist intended it as a pessimistic commentary on all human life, or not, his series of episodes on earth begins and ends with the figure of Vanity. Reading to the left on this same panel one sees a man and a woman starting the journey of life on earth, apparently with suffering but certainly with courage perhaps for the sake of the children they carry.

The West panel now shows the first of three incidents or problems of life on earth. This is entitled Natural Selection. Two women turn to one man who is clearly superior to the two men they are leaving. The two who have been spurned as mates cling to the hands of the women even while they are turning away.

The North panel represents The Survival of the Fittest. Two men are in combat, the woman at the left evidently to be the prize of the victor. At the other side a woman tries to draw away one of the combatants. The sculptor has given this group a second title, "The Awakening of the War Spirit," which is equally applicable.

The East panel is entitled The Lesson of Life. A young man and a young woman turn to each other through natural impulse, while an older woman with the experience of life attempts to counsel them.

On the other side an old man restrains an impetuous youth who evidently would fight for the girl.

Turning the corner now to the South panel again, there are two figures representing Lust trying to embrace a reluctant woman. Then one comes to Vanity once more, and the story of life on earth is done. Again there is a gap, and the scene leaves the earth for the unknown world after physical death.

The East face of the minor group first shows the figure of Greed, with his worldly goods now turned literally to a ball of clay in his hands, gazing back at earth in puzzlement. The next two figures show Faith offering the hope of immortality (as symbolized in the scarab) as consolation to a sorrowing woman. Finally there are two figures sinking back into Oblivion, drawn by the hand of Destiny. Thus the cycle from Oblivion through life and back to Oblivion is completed.

In the same basin, at the far south end, is a figure of The Setting Sun. This was part of the artist's conception of the Fountain of Earth, the relation to the main group being found in the supposition that the earth is a mass thrown off by the sun. Thus is emphasized the idea that the earth and life on earth are but a very small part of the wider unknown universe and life.

At the four corners of the main composition of the fountain, separating the four panels, are Hermae, terminal pillars such as the Greeks and Romans were fond of, decorated with the head of Hermes, god of boundaries.

Having worked out the story, it is well to go back to appreciate the purely aesthetic qualities of the fountain. Note especially the feeling of strength in the figures, the firm modeling, and the fine way in which the figures are grouped. The composition of the west face of the minor monument is especially fine, and the very graceful lines here make an intimate appeal that is not evident in some of the other groups. The whole monument is austere and strongly compelling rather than intimately charming. If it is the first duty of art to make people think, this is the most successful bit of sculpture on the grounds.

Mural Paintings

The mural paintings in, the Court of Abundance consist of eight panels by Frank Brangwyn, perhaps the greatest living mural decorator, placed in the four corners of the cloister. Though not entirely in key with the color scheme and not an integral part of the court as a whole, these are distinctly the works of a master. Ultra-learned critics will tell you that they fail as decorations, since they are interesting as individual pictures rather than as panels heightening the architectural charm. But their placing shows clearly that there was no intention that they should appear as part of the architectural scheme. It is better to accept them as pictures, forgetting the set standards by which one ordinarily judges mural painting.

The eight paintings represent the elements: two panels each for Fire, Earth, Air and Water. There are no conventional figures here personifying the elements, but scenes from the life of intensely human people, typifying the uses to which man has put the elements.

Fire. Beginning on the tower side of the court, at the northeast corner, are the two panels representing Fire. The one on the north wall is called "Primitive Fire." A group of figures surround a fire, some nursing it and some holding out their hands to the heat, while a man at the back brings fagots. Note the color accents in the robes of the three standing figures.

"Industrial Fire," on the east wall, represents the bringing of fire into the service of man. In some particulars this is among the finest of the paintings, but the transverse cloud of smoke seems to break it awkwardly.

Earth is represented in the two panels in the northwest corner. The one on the north wall is entitled "The Fruit Pickers," typifying the wealth of products that man obtains from the earth. This is perhaps the richest of the panels, in the profusion of color and of alluring form.

The panel on the west wall is "The Dancing of the Grapes," a variation of the theme of "The Fruit Pickers." It tells the story of the grape: above are the pickers and the harvesters with baskets; at the right two figures dancing to crush the juices from the grapes; and in the foreground a group with the finished wine. The confusion of figures at first is puzzling; but viewed simply as a spotting of bright colors there is no finer panel among them all. It is better to stand well back along the colonnade, and forgetting the subject, to delight in the purely sensuous impression.

Air is represented in the two panels in the southwest corner. The one on the south wall is called "The Hunters." The theme is suggested in the idea of the arrows fleeing on the wings of the air, and also by the flight of birds above.

The panel on the west wall is called "The Windmill." Note how the feeling of moving air is suggested everywhere: in the skies at the back, in the clouds and the kites, in the trees and the grain-field, in the draperies, and even in the figures themselves that are braced against the wind. The coloring is glorious, and the composition fine. The disposition of masses of light and dark is notable the dark figures grouped against the golden grain, and the gold-brown windmill against the dark sky. No panel in the grounds will better repay intensive study.

Water is represented in the panels of the southwest corner of the court. The one on the south wall is called "The Net," and typifies the wealth that man draws from the water. A group of fishermen are hauling in a net, and carriers bring baskets at the back.

"The Fountain," the panel on the east wall, shows a group of people who have come to fill their jars at a spring. The colors here are softer, though quite as rich as elsewhere. The lower half of the painting is, indeed, like a richly colored mosaic.

After examining "The Fountain" at close range it is well to step back to the middle of this south corridor. Look first at "The Windmill" and then turn to look again at "The Fountain." Note, how, when the subjects are once understood, the great distance increases rather than decreases the charm of the paintings. Note especially how beautiful each one is when considered merely as a pattern of color. These two panels, if not the finest of all, at least must take rank among the best three or four.

The North Court of Abundance

Passing under the tower from the Court of Abundance one comes out in the little north court that is conceived in the same spirit, and which likewise is dominated by the Mullgardt tower. The architecture here is like an echo of that of the main court, the decorated spaces alternating with bare spaces. The tower sculptures are all repeated on this side. The only sculpture within the north court is Sherry Fry's personification of Aquatic Life. The statue is of a heavy sort that should be anywhere but in this place of ethereal mood and exquisite detailed workmanship. Blot out the background and you can see that the figure has a certain solid grace. But if designed for this court it fails of its decorative purpose.

Court of the Universe

The Court of the Universe is the most magnificent of the courts. Considering the many units-the noble arches, the long colonnades with their corner pavilions, the sunken garden with its fountains and decorative sculpture, and the vista to the Column of Progress and the Marina-it is by far the richest in artistic interest. But is it so imposing, so vast, that it necessarily lacks the sense of quiet restfulness and intimacy of appeal of the smaller courts. It is in a sense the Civic Center of the great Exposition model city, and as such it offers many suggestions of wise planning-and one or two of poor planning, as in the case of the obtrusive band-stand.

The meaning of the court is to be found in the symbolism of the groups surmounting the two triumphal arches-the Nations of the East meeting the Nations of the West. With the opening of the Panama Canal the peoples of the universe have met at last; West faces East on this shore of the Pacific. The idea is finely expressed in the lines by Walt Whitman, inscribed on the west arch, in which the spirit of the Aryan race, having traveled this far, is supposed to speak as she gazes westward to Asia, "the house of maternity," her original home:

> Facing west from California's shores,
> Inquiring, tireless, seeking what is yet unfound,
> I, a child, very old, over waves, towards the house
>   of maternity, the land of migrations, look afar,
> Look off the shores of my Western Sea,
>   the circle almost circled.

Variations of this theme may be found in the murals under the arches, and in those under the Tower of Jewels near by. Other universal themes are treated in the Fountains of the Rising Sun and of the Setting Sun, and in The Elements at the edge of the sunken garden. The idea of achievement, of victory in conquering the universe, is also suggested in the triumphal arches.

Architecture

The style of architecture is in general Roman; though, as is true almost throughout the Exposition buildings, there is an admixture of Renaissance motives. Even on the massive Roman arches there is a trace of Moorish lightness and color in the green lattices; and the domes of the corner pavilions are clearly Eastern in feeling.

The East and West arches are, of course, reminiscent of the triumphal arches of the Roman Conquerors. A comparison with pictures of the famous Arch of Constantine and the Arch of Titus at Rome, will show how thoroughly the architects have mastered the feeling of the classic examples, while largely modifying the decorative features. To properly see either of the arches in this court as a single unit, it is best to stand at the side of the sunken garden, near one of the figures of "The Elements," where the fountain columns do not obstruct the view.

The long colonnade, with its fine Corinthian columns and its surmounting row of "Star-girls," can best be appreciated when one stands facing north, with back to the Tower of Jewels-since the architecture of that was clearly conceived by another mind and built in a different spirit. It is from the two corner pavilions on the tower side, perhaps, that the best general views of the court can be obtained. Unfortunately the attractive view down the straight colonnades of the north extension of the court is marred by a gaudy band pavilion, which is quite out of keeping with the pervading mood of simple dignity. The little corner pavilions are worthy of study alone, as a graceful and unusual bit of architectural design.

The Court of the Universe was designed by McKim, Mead and White.

Sculpture

The Court of the Universe has more than its share of the best sculpture of the Exposition. In this court more than anywhere else one can obtain an idea of the remarkable scope of the sculptured groups. It is a good place to linger in if one has heretofore had pessimistic doubts about the ultimate flowering of the art of sculpture in America.

The Fountain of the Rising Sun is at the east end of the sunken garden. Its tall shaft is surmounted by the figure of a youth typifying the Rising Sun-a figure of irresistible appeal. The morning of day and the morning of life, the freshness of the dawn and the aspiration of youth— these things are remarkably suggested in the figure. With head up and winged arms outstretched, the youth is poised on tiptoe, the weight thrown forward, as if just on the point of soaring.

The Fountain of the Setting Sun is just opposite, at the west end of the sunken garden. The surmounting figure here, though officially called "The Setting Sun," is more appropriately named "Descending Night"-the title the artist has given to the bronze replica in the Fine Arts gallery. The closing in of night-that is what is so perfectly suggested in the relaxed body, the folding-in wings, and the remarkable sense of drooping that characterizes the whole statue. There is, too, an enveloping sense of purity and sweetness about the figure.

These two statues which surmount the Fountains of the Rising Sun and the Setting Sun are among the most charming sculptures at the Exposition. They have not the strength of the figures of the Elements, or the massive nobility and repose of the Genius of Creation, or the purely modern native appeal of the works of Stackpole and Young and Fraser. But for those of us who are sculpture lovers without asking why, they come closer to our hearts and dwell more intimately in our minds than any of these. "Descending Night" especially has a sensuous charm of graceful line, a maidenly loveliness, that appeals irresistibly. Both figures are by Adolph A. Weinman.

Above the higher basin of each fountain the column drum is decorated with figures in relief. While the two friezes are meant to be decorative primarily, the artist has employed in each case a symbolism in keeping with the crowning figure. The frieze in the Fountain of the Rising Sun represents "Day Triumphant." The symbolic figures typify the awakening of man's finer instincts and energies at the call of the morning, and the shrinking of the vices when the darkness of night gives place to the light of day. The relief-frieze of the "Fountain of the Setting Sun" is entitled "The Gentle Powers of Night." It represents Descending Night bringing with her the Stars, the Moon-goddess, Dreams, and similar beautiful things. The lower basins of both fountains contain figures of centaurs (a new sea-variety, with fins) holding sea-monsters.

Groups surmounting arches. The monumental groups surmounting the two triumphal arches are "The Nations of the East," on the Arch of the Rising Sun, and "The Nations of the West," on the Arch of the Setting Sun. The symbolic idea behind the two compositions thus placed facing each other, is that of the nations of the Eastern and Western Hemispheres at last meeting on this Pacific shore.

The Nations of the East is made up of five mounted and four unmounted figures, all typical of the Orient. Reading from the spectator's left to right, the mounted figures are: 1. an Arab tribal chief on a horse; 2. a Mohammedan standard bearer on a camel; 3. the East Indian on his richly-caparisoned elephant; 4. another Mohammedan standard-bearer on a camel; 5. a Mongolian horseman. Between the mounted figures are the following on foot: 1. a servant with a basket of fruits; 2. an Arab falconer; 3. a Thibetan lama or priest; 4. another servant with fruit.

The Nations of the West represents typical figures from the European nations which have helped to develop America, together with two American Indians and an Alaskan. A central composition shows the Mother of Tomorrow and a surmounting group typifying the Spirit of Enterprise which has led the Aryan race to conquer the West. The figures, from left to right, are: 1. the French-Canadian (sometimes called "The Trapper"), on horseback; 2. the Alaskan, carrying totem poles, on foot; 3. the Spanish-American conqueror, mounted; 4. the German-American, on foot; 5. the Mother of Tomorrow, on the tongue of the ox-drawn prairie schooner; 6. the Italian-American, on foot; 7. the English-American, mounted; 8. an Indian squaw; 9. the American Indian, mounted. On top of the prairie schooner the Spirit of Enterprise is represented by a spirited winged figure, with a boy at either hand.

The way in which the two groups balance each other at the two ends of the court is worthy of study-the elephant of the one offset by the prairie schooner of the other. Indeed each feature of one is balanced in the other so that the two will mass against the sky with the same general decorative effect. "The Nations of the East," considered as a whole, seems the more satisfying group-richer in feeling, more unified in design, and more massive; in short, more monumental and therefore better fitted to crown the noble arch. But if this fits its setting better, and masses against the sky more satisfyingly, "The Nations of the West" will be found on close examination to contain the better individual figures. The Alaskan (unfortunately almost lost to view in the present placing of the group), the Canadian Trapper, and the mounted Indian are all worthy of prolonged study; and the figure of the Mother of Tomorrow is one of the finest bits of sculpture at the Exposition. In these figures, and only slightly less so in the other figures of this and the opposite group, there is ample evidence that the American sculptors have outgrown the traditions of by-gone "schools" and have developed a genuine native medium of expression. The two groups are the work of A. Stirling Calder, Leo Lentelli, and Frederick G. R. Roth in collaboration.

Figures at north and south of sunken garden. Flanking the stairways to the sunken garden at north and south are four large figures by Robert Aitken, typifying "The Elements."

Air is at the west end of the south stairway, and is represented as a huge winged female figure putting a star in her hair. Two birds, old-time symbols of the air, complete the suggestion. At the back a man has tied himself to the wings of the figure typifying man's effort to put to his own use the wings of the air.

Earth is placed at the east end of the south stairway. A huge female figure rests on conventionalized rocks, and a formalized tree partially supports her. At the back two small struggling figures are seen, typifying man's struggle with the forces of earth.

Water is placed at the east end of the north stairway. The sea-god, with his trident in one hand and sea-weed in the other, rides on a wave, with a dolphin beside him.

Fire at the west end of the north stairway-is typified by the figure of a man in agony, with one hand grasping the flame, and with jagged lightning in the other, symbolizing man's terror of fire as well as his conquering of it. A salamander completes the main design, while at the back the phoenix, bird fabled to rise from fire, helps support the figure.

These four figures are of the sort of art that is likely to turn the unthinking person away, though a study of them will bring out new beauties with riper acquaintance. Because people fail to get far enough away from them to obtain the proper perspective, the statues seem too huge, too strong, too terrible, ever to be attractive. They are, it is true, out of scale, and thus mar the effect of the court to a certain extent. But there is in them something of the noble and compelling strength of the statues of Michael Angelo-to whom the sculptor clearly owes his inspiration. Stand between the columns at the corner of the Transportation Palace, and you will see that the figure of Fire not only is imaginatively conceived but is a fine line composition as well. Study of the other three from corresponding viewpoints will well repay in increased understanding and pleasure.

Figures at east and west of sunken gardens. Flanking the east and west stairways are two groups by Paul Manship. The one representing two girls dancing or running is called sometimes "Festivity," sometimes "Motion." Here the artist has welded the figures into an ornamental design in a way unparalleled in the work of other American sculptors. Note the finely varied outline, the sense of rhythmic motion, and the rich feeling that every part is decorative. The opposite group is called "Music" or "Music and Poetry." It lacks the flowing grace and something of the richness of feeling of the other, though it is more dignified. There is the same conventionalization in treatment, again charming. These groups are not for people who look for realism in art above all else; but for those who care for the classic, who see in formalization a short-cut to the expression of the spirit of a thing, there are few more appealing groups in the grounds. The figures are repeated at the east and west entrances to the garden.

Minor Sculptures. The slender "Stars" along the top of the colonnade are the work of A. Stirling Calder. When one remembers that this is the Court of the Universe, they seem to fit in with the meaning of the whole, and architecturally their symmetry of form fits them well for repetition. The low relief friezes on the corner pavilions represent "The Signs of the Zodiac," and are by Hermon A. MacNeil. A formalized Atlas is represented in the center, and at each side are seven of his daughters, the Pleiades and the Hyades, whom the gods changed into stars. Twelve of the maidens have plaques bearing the symbols of the Zodiac. The frieze is well composed and beautifully modeled, but the rough Travertine does not do it justice. The minor sculptures on the triumphal arches consist of a repeated winged angel with sword down-turned, by Leo Lentelli; spirited spandrels over the arches, representing "Pegasus," by Frederick G. R. Roth; and two well-adapted medallions by A. Stirling Calder and B. Bufano. All of these decorative features are repeated on both sides of both arches.

Mural Paintings

The four mural paintings of the Court of the Universe, two under each of the triumphal arches, represent the progress of civilization from the old world to the American far West. The two under the Arch of the Rising Sun, at the east of the court, represent the nations that crossed the Atlantic and their ideals, while those under the western arch show the march of the pioneers from New England to California. To obtain the proper sequence of thought the ones under the eastern arch should be examined first.

Murals in Arch of the Rising Sun. On the south wall of the arch is a panel representing the nations that have dared to cross the Atlantic to bring their civilization to America. The figure farthest to the spectator's right represents the spirit of adventure or "The Call to Fortune." Then follow representatives of the nations, in this order: 1. the half-savage of the lost Continent of Atlantis; 2. the Roman conqueror; 3. the Spanish explorer, typified by a figure resembling Columbus; 4. the English explorer, resembling Raleigh; 5. a priest, typifying the bringing of European religion to America; 6. the artist, bringing the arts; and 7. the workman-immigrant of today. Then follows an allegorical veiled figure, with hand to ear, listening to the hopes and ideals of the men who are following the call to fortune.

The opposite panel shows what the veiled figure has heard-depicts the hopes and ideals that have led men to cross the Atlantic. At the far left are figures symbolizing True Hope and False Hope. Soap bubbles are being scattered by False Hope, and the third figure, typifying Adventure, tries to pick them up. Then follow the true ideals and hopes in this order: 1. Commerce 2. Imaginative Inspiration; 3. Truth and Beauty (one figure); 4. Religion; 5. Wealth; and 6. Family joys (a woman with babes). In this panel the background contains suggestions of Asiatic and American cities. In the other panel the background shows a group of ships, ranging from those of the earliest times to the modern liner.

These two paintings are worthy of study for the historical and symbolic interest. Artistically they are notable chiefly for the remarkable freshness of coloring and rich mosaic effect. Both are by Edward Simmons.

Murals in Arch of the Setting Sun, at the west side of the court. The painting on the north wall should be viewed first. This represents pioneers from a New England village starting for California. There are four groups of figures, as follows: 1. two workmen, and a woman holding a child; 2. a symbolic figure of the Call to Fortune; 3. a group showing the types of those who crossed the continent-the driver first, and then the Preacher, the Pioneer, the Judge, and the Schoolmistress (there are four children also in this group, and at the back is a wagon filled with household goods); and 4. a youth bidding farewell to his parents as he starts to join the band of emigrants. At the back of the last group is seen a typical New England home, and in the distance a New England meeting-house.

"The Arrival on the Pacific Coast" is the title of the painting on the opposite wall, which represents the immigrants being welcomed as they reach California. Here again there are four groups of figures. The first shows two Spanish-American soldiers and their captain, following a priest, typical of the days of Spanish rule in California and of the Mission period. Second, there is a symbolic figure, "The Spirit of Enlightenment." The third and main group shows types of immigrants. The men here are: 1. the scientist; 2. the architect; 3. the writer; 4. the sculptor; 5. the painter; 6. the agriculturist; and 7. the miner (or other manual worker). A woman and several children complete the group, and at the back is a prairie schooner, from which a girl waves a flag. The fourth group represents California welcoming the immigrants, the state being symbolized by tokens of the wealth it has to offer settlers: the orange tree, sheaves of grain, and fruits-the figures including the miner, the farmer, fruit pickers, and the California bear. This last group is the most colorful, and in many ways the most appealing, of all those in the two panels under the west arch. It is interesting to compare the golden warmth here and indeed throughout the California panel-with the cold atmosphere of the New England one.

Those who are familiar with the historical characters of the West will be able to recognize in the California panel idealized portraits of William Keith as the painter, Bret Harte as the writer, and Junipero Serra as the priest. In the New England panel may be found William Taylor, famous street preacher of the early days in California, as the preacher, and "Grizzly" Adams as the pioneer.

Both murals under the Arch of the Setting Sun are by Frank Vincent Dumond.

The Side Courts

The two small connecting courts, or aisles, at the east and west of the Court of the Universe are known as the Florentine Court and the Venetian Court respectively. Both are in Italian Renaissance architecture, and both are remarkably rich in color. The patterns on the shafts of the columns, while doubtless adding to the feeling of richness, are a little too pronounced, tending to destroy that restfulness which is felt in the other Italian courts, the Court of Flowers and the Court of Palms. In both the Florentine Court and the Venetian Court the planting schemes harmonize unusually well with the architecture.

-

Size of the Court of the Universe

For the sake of those who find added interest in knowing on what scale a work of art is built, the following facts are added:

The area of the Court of the Universe is about seven acres. On its east and west axis, from arch to arch, it is six hundred and fifty feet; on its north and south axis, from the Tower of Jewels to the Column of Progress, it is nearly twelve hundred feet.

The Arches of the Rising Sun and the Setting Sun have a total height, to the top of the surmounting sculpture, of two hundred and three feet.

The Tower of Jewels is 433 feet in height, while the main archway beneath is 110 feet high.

Court of the Four Seasons

The Court of the Four Seasons, unlike the other main courts, does not immediately call forth one's exclamations of surprise and delight. It is not so compellingly beautiful as either of the others. Nevertheless it has a distinctive charm of its own-a reposeful atmosphere and a simplicity of form that become more and more appealing with riper acquaintance. It is a good place to come to when one is satiated with the beauties of the other courts, for restfulness is the keynote. The simple massive style of the architecture and the simple planting scheme combine to produce a spirit of calm. The ideas of energy, achievement, progress, effort-so insistently emphasized elsewhere-are left behind, and everything breathes a sense of peace and orderliness, of things happening all in good season.

The primary idea underlying the decorative features of the court is sufficiently indicated in the name, "The Four Seasons;" and this idea is symbolically expressed in the sculpture and mural paintings in the four corners of the colonnade. But a study of the other decorations shows that the idea of abundance, or fruitfulness, was equally in the minds of architect and sculptors. The purely architectural ornaments, such as the capitals and the running borders, employ the symbols of agriculture and fruitfulness, while no less than five of the main sculptural groups or figures deal directly with harvest themes.

Architecture

The style of architecture is in general Roman. The half-dome and the colonnades are almost severely classic. The column capitals are Ionic. But in the freedom of some of the architectural forms, particularly in the archways at east and west, there is a suggestion of Renaissance influence. The plan with its four cut-corners with fountains, and its half-dome facing down the long colonnade to the bay, is ingenious. The half-dome itself, dominating feature of the court, is exceptionally dignified and impressive. To obtain the best view of it as a single unit, one should stand between two columns of the colonnade near either the Fountain of Summer or the Fountain of Autumn-as from these points the eye is not carried through the doorway at the back of the dome, to the detriment of a unified impression.

Henry Bacon is the architect who designed the Court of the Four Seasons.

Sculpture

Bulls on pylons. The finest sculpture here is to be found in the groups capping the pylons at the entrance to the minor north court. Though called by the artist "The Feast of Sacrifice," these are commonly known as "The Bulls." The group, which is duplicated, shows a bull being led to sacrifice by a youth and a maid, and is reminiscent of the harvest-time celebrations of ancient peoples. But it is just as well to forget the subject, and to admire purely for the sensuous charm-for the beauty of outline, the fine modeling, and the remarkable sense of spirited action. Note the three figures individually: the nobly animated bull, the magnificently set-up youth, and the strong yet graceful maiden; then note how the sacrificial garland holds the whole group together and makes it richer. Note, too, how the forward-moving lines of the bull are accentuated on one side by the similar lines of the youth's body, and on the other by the contrasting lines of the girl's. Putting aside any question of meaning, there is not in any of the courts a nobler bit of decorative work than this. Albert Jaegers was the sculptor.

Figures surmounting columns. On the two columns before the half-dome are Albert Jaegers' figures of "Rain" and "Sunshine." At the right, as one faces the dome, Rain is typified by a woman shielding her head with her mantle and holding out a shell to catch the water. At the left Sunshine is represented by a woman shielding her head from the sun's rays with a palm-branch. Both figures are characterized by a sense of richness, of fullness, that is perfectly in keeping with the spirit of the court. In commenting on these statues, in one of his lectures on the art of the Exposition, Eugen Neuhaus, the well-known California painter, suggested very appropriately that the court should have been named for them "The Court of the Two

Seasons" since in California the only noticeable seasonal change is from a sunny period to a rainy period.

Group surmounting half-dome. This shows a conventional seated figure of Harvest, with an overflowing cornucopia. At one side a child-figure bows under a load of fruit. This group also is by Albert Jaegers. Here, as in "Rain" and "Sunshine," there is a sense of fruitfulness, of profuseness, a maternal suggestion that helps to carry out the symbolism of the court. In all three of these statues, too, there is something of the nobility and massiveness that distinguish the same artist's "bull" groups across the court. All are eminently suited to the massive Roman architecture; nowhere else have sculptor and architect worked together more successfully.

Fountains of the Seasons. In the niches formed at the corners of the court by the diagonal colonnades are novel fountains, surmounted by groups representing the four seasons. It is well to go first to the southwest corner, to the "Fountain of Spring"; then to the northwest corner, for "Summer"; and so on around the court. If one is ever puzzled to understand from the figures which season is represented, a glance at the labeled murals up above in the corridor will give the proper title for statue and murals of each season are grouped together.

Spring. A young woman draws a floral garland over her head, while at her right a love-lorn youth turns a pleading face to her, and at her left a girl brings armfuls of flowers.

Summer. To a man a woman holds up a babe, symbol of the summer of human life, while at one side a crouching figure holds a sheaf of full-headed grain.

Autumn. The central figure is a woman of generous build with a jar on her shoulder-quite the usual personification of Autumn or fruitfulness. At one side a young woman holds a garland of grapes, and at the other is a girl with a babe. This last figure is perhaps the most graceful in all the four groups, though the same sort of loveliness distinguishes to a certain extent the two flower-girls of "Spring." Altogether, this "Autumn" fountain is probably the finest of the four.

Winter. The central figure is Nature, in the nakedness of winter, resting after the harvests of autumn and waiting for the birth of spring. At one side a man with a spade rests, while on the other a man with a seed-bag is already beginning to sow. Although all the figures of "The Fountains of the Seasons" are nude, there is about this group a sense of cold nakedness that well accords with the season it portrays.

These four groups are very properly alike in composition and feeling-suggesting perhaps that the differences between the seasons in California are but slight. There is throughout a conventional touch, and all are in pastoral mood. The groups are by Furio Piccirilli.

The Fountain of Ceres is in the north extension of the court, between the Palace of Food Products and the Palace of Agriculture. The surmounting figure is of Ceres, Greek goddess of the fields and especially of corn. The bas-relief frieze represents a group of dancers, suggestive of the seasonal festivals of the Greeks. The main figure has been much criticized, but an unbiased critic may find much in the fountain to praise. The pedestal and the crowning figure are well thought out, and the proportions of the whole are good; and there is a feeling of classic simplicity throughout. The frieze of dancing girls, too, is exceptionally graceful. If, then, one discovers that Ceres is more mature than a goddess ever ought to be, or that her face suggests that of an exasperated school-teacher, or if one finds the cornstalk in her hand a realistic thing incompatible with any poetic conception, it is well to step back until one gets only the general effect. For there is much to admire in the poise of the figure, in the decorative outline, and in the sculptor's lightness of touch. The fountain was designed by Evelyn Beatrice Longman.

Minor Sculptures. On the archways at east and west of the court a high-relief figure by August Jaegers is repeated eight times, and the spandrels over the arches are by the same artist. In both cases the idea of abundance or fruitfulness again supplies the motive. The boxes at the bases of the columns on which "Rain" and "Sunshine" stand are decorated with agricultural scenes in low relief. The capitals at the tops of these columns are enriched with groups of agricultural figures. Within the archways at east and west the ceilings are decorated with delicate bas-relief designs, patterned after the famous ones at Villa Maderna, Rome.

Mural Paintings

All the murals in the Court of the Four Seasons are by H. Milton Bancroft. In general they are less interesting than those of any other court.

The Seasons. In the four corners of the colonnade there are eight panels, grouped by twos as follows: Spring and Seed Time; Summer and Fruition; Autumn and Harvest; and Winter and Festivity. There is little to hold the attention either in richness of color or in unusual grace of composition. Moreover, the artist has left nothing to the imagination in the symbolism by which he expresses the several ideas. The devices are so hackneyed, and the meaning so obvious, that any sort of interpretation would be entirely superfluous.

Panels under half-dome. On the east wall under the dome is the panel Art Crowned by Time. Father Time crowns Art, while on one side stand figures representing Weaving, Jewelry, and Glasswork, and on the other Printing, Pottery, and Smithery. On the opposite wall is the panel Man Receiving Instruction in Nature's Laws. A woman holds before a babe a tablet inscribed "Laws of Nature," while on one side are figures of Fire, Earth and Water, and on the other figures of Death, Love, and Life. These two larger panels are more pleasing than the eight representing the Seasons, both in coloring and in figure composition; and they make pleasing spots of bright color in the dome. But again the artist is tediously careful to make his meanings plain. Not only does each figure hold its obvious symbol prominently in view, but there are labels naming the figures. To the art student the painter's stipple-and-line method, producing vibration of light and a certain freshness of atmosphere, will be of interest, as being out of the usual run of mural technique.

Before leaving the Court of the Four Seasons one should stand under the central arch of the triple portal at the east, and look first to the east through the Arch of the Setting Sun to the group "Nations of the East;" and then to the west along the vista that ends with the kneeling figure before the Fine Arts temple. The arrangement of architectural and sculptural units in both vistas is worthy of study.

The Court of Palms and the Court of Flowers

In these two courts, which pierce the walled city on the south, opposite the Palace of Horticulture and opposite Festival Hall, is to be found the purest expression of that spirit of the Italian Renaissance which hovers over so much of the Exposition architecture. Here, too, one finds Jules Guerin's color scheme at its richest. Both courts necessarily lack the cloistral charm of the Court of Abundance, since they have the fourth sides open. But what they lack in the sense of enclosure they make up in sunniness and joyous color. They are restful and warm and quiet-and artistically they are among the most perfect and most harmonious units on the grounds.

The Court of Palms

The Court of Palms is directly opposite the Palace of Horticulture, between the Education and Liberal Arts Palaces, and adjoins the Court of the Four Seasons. The charming sunken garden and simple pool reflect the colored colonnade, arches and towers with a sense of rest that is a relief and stimulant after walking miles of exhibit halls. Although really nearly two acres in area, the court seems small and intimate. The proportions are good, and the planting particularly fortunate.

The architecture is Renaissance, and is suggestive of the interior courts of the palaces of the Italian nobles. The colonnade columns are Ionic. The high attic story or frieze above the colonnade is remarkably rich, with its orange brown panels garlanded with green and red fruits, and decorated with Caryatid pilasters. It is worthy of study for the way in which architect, sculptor and color director have co-operated. The Italian Towers, terminating the colonnades, are among the finest bits of architectural design in the whole building group. Though only a fraction of the height of the Tower of Jewels, they convey much better the impression of reaching high into the heavens, of aspiration and uplift. They are more satisfying, too, in their combination of architectural forms, and they carry out notably well the delicate but luxuriant color scheme of the court. The unusual repeated pattern which fills the large wall panels of the towers is worthy of attention.

The architect of the court was George W. Kelham.

Sculpture. The only really important statue in the court is that which stands at the opening on the Avenue of Palms-called The End of the Trail. An Indian, bowed at last under the storm, sits astride a dejected horse utter weariness, discouragement, lost hope, expressed in every line of man and animal. Some see in the statue only the abject despair of a horse and rider when the consciousness finally comes that the trail is definitely lost in the wilderness; and it is notable enough as an expression of this tragic theme. But others, remembering the history of the Indian, see here an eloquent and pathetic reminder of a race that has seemingly come to the end of its trail. As a portrayal of this racial tragedy the group is even more remarkable than as an expression of the hopelessness of a lost man and horse.

The statue is hardly in key with its architectural surroundings; but its comparatively isolated position prevents it from seeming an intrusive element in the court. Considered alone it is more individual, more expressive of independent and deep moving thought, than any other sculpture in the grounds. There is far more of real earnestness here than is usual in exposition sculpture. The thing is significant, too, for the native note. It is worthy of serious study as indicating one of the most important tendencies of American sculpture when not tied to the purely decorative. The sculptor was James Earl Fraser.

The minor sculptures in this court consist of the Caryatides by John Bateman and A. Stirling Calder; the spandrels, by Albert Weinert; "The
Fairy," by Carl Gruppe, which crowns the Italian Towers; and the classic
vases at the portals.

The mural paintings in this court are disappointing. Two are surprisingly poor, considering the high reputation of the artists, and the third is badly placed. The tympanum in the portal at the east side of the court is filled by Charles W. Holloway's panel, The Pursuit of Pleasure. This is a conventional treatment of the subject, in which a number of youths and maidens turn lackadaisically to a winged figure of Pleasure. There is a pleasing lightness of touch, and the bright reds and blues are in keeping with the spirit of the court-but the thing is, somehow, insipid. This panel is more pleasing under illumination. In the opposite portal is Childe Hassam's painting, Fruits and Flowers. This again is a conventional treatment, showing very obviously vegetable and human fruits and flowers. The arrangement is tediously symmetric, the coloring is rather weak, and there is a wooden stiffness about the figures. The panel makes a pleasant spot of color, but is by no means up to the standard of the canvases in Hassam's room in the Palace of Fine Arts.

The panel over the main doorway, at the north end of the court, is by Arthur F. Mathews, and is far superior to the other two, though unfortunately placed in a dark spot. It is called by the artist A Victorious Spirit. The central figure, gorgeously suggesting the Spirit of Enlightment, protects Youth from the discordant elements of life from materialism and brute force, as represented by the rearing horse and militant rider. Youth is attended by the peace-bringing elements of life, by Religion, Philosophy or Education, and the Arts. The symbolism here is sound, the composition and drawing unusually good, and the coloring quite wonderful-especially in the orange-yellow robe of the Spirit. The full deep colors are in sharp contrast with those of most of the Exposition murals.

No one should leave this court without first pausing to enjoy the vista through the north doorway, showing Albert Jaeger's spirited Sacrificial Bulls on the Agriculture and Food Products Palaces, the long colonnade of the Court of the Four Seasons, and the bit of bay and hills beyond.

The Court of Flowers

The Court of Flowers is opposite to Festival Hall, between the Mines and Varied Industries Palaces. The first impression, as one comes to it, is that here is a replica of the colorful Court of Palms. But many differences become evident after a few moments' study.

The architecture is Italian Renaissance, but of a more richly decorative sort than in the Court of Palms. There is more overlaid ornament, and on the whole, less simplicity and quietness and more varied interest. The columns here are Corinthian, arranged in pairs. The gallery above the colonnade adds to the suggestion of the sunny South. The Italian Towers, while similar in feeling to those of the other court, are different in the arrangement of elements, though equally successful. The color decoration is again notable.

It is hardly necessary to add that George W. Kelham designed this court too.

Sculpture. The center of the court is dominated by Edgar Walter's Beauty and the Beast Fountain. The surmounting statue is a curious combination of graceful lines and grotesque effects. The strange Beast is no less fantastic than the young lady herself-she who has adorned her fair body with nothing more than a Spring hat and a pair of sandals. It is probably this near-nudeness, without pure nakedness, that creates the jarring note of the group Certainly there is a bizarre touch that somewhat offsets the sinuous charm of the figure. Under the upper basin are four piping Pans, not notable individually, but adding to the decorative effect. The wall around the lower pool carries a playful frieze of animals in low relief.

The Pioneer is the title of the equestrian statue at the south end of the court, on the Avenue of Palms. The man is typically the Western pioneer, as every resident of the Pacific Coast has known him-a patriarchal figure who foreran civilization here in the West of America as he has in all other new lands. Head up, axe and gun in hand, looking straight forward, he is a fine visualization of the "Forty-niner." He is, too, an interesting racial contrast to the Indian of "The End of the Trail." One wonders, however, about the horse, with the elaborate trappings that clearly belong to another era-to the days of Spanish conquest, perhaps. Certainly horse and rider do not seem to be conceived in the same spirit. The group lacks, too, that vital intensity of feeling and that emotional strength which distinguish "The End of the Trail," the companion-statue in the Court of Palms. The "Pioneer" is by Solon Borglum.

The minor sculpture here consists of A. Stirling Calder's attractive "Flower Girl," repeated in the niches along the loggia; dignified Lions,
by Albert Laessle, flanking the three portals; and again Carl

Gruppe's
"The Fairy," atop the Italian Towers.

42

The Tower of Jewels, and the Fountain of Energy

It was planned that the Tower of Jewels should be the great dominating feature of the architectural scheme of the Exposition; that this unit more than any other should stand as a triumphal monument to celebrate the opening of the Panama Canal. The mural paintings, the sculpture and the inscriptions all carry out this idea, but the tower, in its architectural aspect alone, fails to live up fully to its purpose. It serves well to "center" the whole scheme, and to afford an imposing pile at the main entrance. Nevertheless it falls short of the high architectural standard of the courts and palaces.

Architecture

The architectural forms used in the design of the tower are in general classic; but the architect has shown considerable originality in their arrangement and massing.

The lower portion, embracing the imposing arch and flanking colonnades, is very dignified and quite satisfying. Standing close to the structure, on the south side, so that one is conscious chiefly of this lower portion, there comes the proper sense of nobility-the feeling that one obtains from a successful triumphal arch. The chief fault of the tower above is that it lacks the long lifting lines that would give a sense of aspiration. It seems just a little squat and fat-as if it were too heavy on top and splayed out at the sides and bottom. It is also somewhat "showy," with too much hung-on ornament; and the green columns against red walls are not satisfying-this being one of the very few failures of the color scheme in the entire group of buildings.

At night the tower takes on a new and unexpected beauty. The outline softens under the illumination, and the feeling of over-decoration and broken lines is lost. The whole structure becomes a huge finger of light, reaching up into the dark heavens-with softer indirect lighting below, and glowing brilliantly above. Even the hundred thousand pendent jewels, which at best are but flashy in the day time, add to the exquisite fairy like effect at night. The illumination here is such, indeed, that it must be one of the most impressive and lasting memories to be carried away by the visitor.

The Tower of Jewels was designed by Thomas Hastings, of the firm Carrere and Hastings of New York.

Sculpture

The sculpture, like the mural paintings, deals in general with the winning of the Americas and the achievement of the canal project.

Sculpture on the tower. As one stands in the South Gardens facing the tower, one sees above the first cornice, reading from left to right, four statues of The Adventurer, The Priest, The Philosopher, and The Soldier. These finely realized figures, which are by John Flanagan, represent four types of the early conquerors of America. On the next story is a repeated equestrian statue of the Spanish Conqueror, called The Armored Horseman, by F. M. L. Tonetti. These five statues are repeated on the other three faces of the tower. There is much other sculpture of a purely decorative sort, the motives used being those usually found in triumphal monuments, such as eagles, wreaths, and the beaks of ships with which the Romans ornamented the columns celebrating their naval successes.

Equestrian statues at entrance. In front of the two side colonnades are spirited equestrian statues. As one faces the tower, the figure at the left is of Pizarro, who conquered the richest portion of South America for Spain. This figure is heroically decorative, and is by Charles Carey Rumsey. At the other side of the main arch is Charles Niehaus' vigorous statue of Cortez, who won Mexico for Spain. This figure, carrying a flag and pennon on a lance, and perfectly seated on the strong horse, has a live sense of movement, and the whole group is informed with the spirit of the lordly conqueror.

Fountains under the tower. Within the colonnades to east and west of the main archway are respectively the Fountain of Youth and the Fountain of El Dorado.

The Fountain of Youth consists of a central figure on a pedestal, and two rounded side panels with figures in relief. Youth is symbolized as a girl, an immature figure, beautifully modeled. She stands, perfectly poised, among rising blossoms. On the pedestal are more flowers in relief, and two dimly indicated half-figures of a man and woman may be discovered. The side panels show old people being drawn away in ships manned by cherubs-old people who gaze back wistfully at the Youth they are leaving. Really the fountain is far more charming if one forgets all but the central figure. There is in that a sweet tenderness, a maidenly loveliness, that makes it the perfect embodiment of Youth-an embodiment to be remembered with delight again and again.

The fountain was designed by Edith Woodman Burroughs.

The Fountain of El Dorado is on the other side of the archway, and is by Gertrude Vanderbilt Whitney. It represents, as a whole, mankind's pursuit of the unattainable. The legend of El Dorado is that there once lived in South America a prince, "The Gilded One," who had so much gold that daily he had his body covered with gold dust. Many Spanish explorers spent fruitless years in search of the fabulously rich country of this prince. The idea of the fountain is that the Gilded One, representing the unattainable, the advantages of wealth and power which deluded men and women seek without value given to the world in return, has just disappeared through the gateway, the gates closing after him. On either side processions of seekers who have glimpsed the Gilded One, strain toward the gateway. Some loiter in love or play, some drop from fatigue, some fight their way along; and the first two, finding that the pursuit is fruitless after all, have dropped to their knees in anguish. The two standing figures beside the gates are said by the sculptor to have no significance beyond the fact that they are "just guardians."

The fountain is notable for its symbolism and for the modeling of the many nude figures. The panel on the right is especially decorative, and has some notably fine individual figures and groups. The spirit of the fountain, with its realism and its note of hopelessness, is not in keeping with that pervading most of the Exposition sculpture. After looking at the work for a time, turn and look back through the two archways at the central figure of Youth at the other side. Certainly no figure in the Fountain of El Dorado has the appeal and charm of that.

Mural Paintings

On the walls of the archway under the Tower of Jewels are eight paintings celebrating the building of the Canal. All are by William de Leftwich Dodge.

On the west wall the first panel is called Discovery. It portrays the discovery of the Pacific Ocean by Balboa.

The second panel is called Atlantic and Pacific. A huge figure of Labor, having brought together the oceans, is opening a waterway from West to East. On the left an ox-drawn prairie schooner has arrived at the shore, with types of Western civilization. On the opposite shore types of the nations of the East, in a colorful group, are straining forward to meet the West.

The third panel is entitled The Purchase. A figure representing the United States is taking over the canal project from France. The French laborers are throwing down their tools, and Americans press forward to take them up.

In the group on the opposite wall the first panel is called Labor Crowned. Victorious Labor is being crowned by the angel of Success, while soldier and workers come to pay homage.

The second panel is entitled The Gateway of All Nations. Figures symbolizing Progress call the world to pass through the Canal. Neptune holds garlands by which he draws ships of the various nations toward the waterway. Two laborers rest on their machines and watch the procession which they have made possible.

The last panel is called Achievement. A woman with the symbols of knowledge, or wisdom, sits enthroned, while about her are grouped figures representing the forces instrumental in building the Canal. At the left are laborers; at the right figures typifying Engineering, Medical Science (with the Caduceus, the wand of Mercury, god of medicine), and Commerce or Munificence.

These mural paintings are among the most interesting and most imaginative of all those at the Exposition. Some of the groups are particularly fine in coloring. Note the method of obtaining the right effect of "flatness" by employing a conventional diaper pattern for the background throughout. The panels here are much more effective under full illumination at night than by daylight.

The Fountain of Energy

The Fountain of Energy in the South Gardens was designed to be the crowning feature of the sculpture of the Exposition, just as the Tower of Jewels was designed to dominate the architectural scheme; and it fails of its high purpose in much the same way. It is closely allied with the tower in symbolic meaning, celebrating man's victory over the forces of nature in the successful building of the canal.

In the pool at the base of the fountain are a number of graceful groups of water sprites on dolphins, and four larger groups representing the four great seas. The one to the east of the main fountain represents The Atlantic Ocean as a woman with sea-horses in one hand and coral like hair, on the back of a conventionalized dolphin. At the north The North Sea is represented by a sort of sea-man, with occasional fins and with a three-pronged spear in hand, riding on a walrus. At the west The Pacific Ocean is typified by a woman on a remarkable sea monster. And on the south a sea-man with negro-like features, and with an octopus in one hand, rides on a sea-elephant, representing The South Seas.

The main pedestal of the statue is a globe, representing the earth. This is supported by a series of figures of mermaids and mermen. The Eastern and Western Hemispheres are represented by figures reclining on the globe, the one to the east a cat-headed woman, the one to the west a bullheaded man. The band, decorated with aquatic figures, which encircles the globe, suggests the final completion of a waterway about the earth.

Energy, the Victor, the surmounting group, typifies the indomitable spirit that has achieved the building of the Canal. The nude figure of Energy with arms outstretched rides a horse through the waves, while on his shoulders stand smaller figures of Valor (with a wreath) and Fame (with a sword) heralding the triumph. These small figures are unfortunate they hardly belong, and instinctively one is worried for their equilibrium.

The whole fountain is instinct with energy, and expresses joyous achievement, as was meant. Moreover it is remarkable in its breadth of conception, in imaginative interpretation of the theme. But it lacks that sense of repose which would make it intimately satisfying.

The fountain was designed by A. Stirling Calder.

Palaces Facing the Avenue of Palms

The adoption of the "walled-city" plan for the Exposition meant the grouping of the more imposing architectural effects in the interior courts, the outer facades simply forming parts of a practically continuous wall about the whole. Inspired by Spanish architecture of the Renaissance, the intention was to keep the wall spaces in general quite bare, concentrating the decorative effects in rich "spots" at carefully chosen intervals. Thus the outer facades of the central group of palaces combine a simple general form with a series of richly ornamental portals. The architect who as entrusted with the designing of the wall and all the portals was W. B. Faville of Bliss and Faville.

Certain architectural and sculptural units are repeated throughout the central group. Each building has a low central dome, seldom seen when one is close to any of the main buildings, but adding greatly to the decorative effect from a slight distance. These domes are of Byzantine style, and are colored in harmonizing shades of green and pink. The small repeated corner domes add another Eastern touch, and are especially effective at night. The outer wall is edged all the way around with a simple cornice and a few rows of dull red tiles, distinctly Southern in feeling, and therefore harmonizing with both the Spanish and the Italian Renaissance doorways.

The Winged Victory is the fine decorative figure that crowns the gables of all the palaces of the walled-city. It is broadly modelled, massive and yet refined, and from any viewpoint stands out in beautiful silhouette against the sky. It is by Louis Ulrich.

Palace of Varied Industries

Before turning to the more important south facade, it is well to look at the east wall, with its dignified and colorful portal. This is Roman in style of architecture, to harmonize with the Palace of Machinery opposite. It is similar in general form to the memorial arches and gateways of the Romans, but in the use of architectural motives and in decoration it is of Italian Renaissance style. The niches at each end of the gallery contain figures of The Miner, by Albert Weinert. The facade is ornamented with buttresses at regular intervals, carrying figures of the California Bear holding a scutcheon with the state seal.

Returning to the Avenue of Palms and the south facade, one sees the most important artistic feature of the building, the central portal. This is a copy, except for the figures filling the niches, of the famous doorway of the Hospital of Santa Cruz at Toledo, Spain. It is in Spanish Renaissance style, of that especially rich type known as "Plateresque," due to its likeness to the work of the silversmiths of the time. For its grace of composition, its exquisite detail, its total effect of richness and depth, this portal is worthy of long study.

The sculpture of the portal is all by Ralph Stackpole. In the lower niches are replicas of "The Man with a Pick," a figure that has been justly admired as a sincere portrayal of a simple laboring type. The relief panel in the tympanum represents various types of industry. From left to right the figures typify Spinning, Building, and Agriculture (or the clothing, sheltering and feeding of mankind), and Manual Labor, and Commerce. The group in the niche above the arch shows a young laborer taking the load from the shoulders of an old man. The single figure at the top of the arch shows the laborer thinking, and is called "Power." Note how all these sculptures, while having individual interest, fit unobtrusively into the lace-like portal.

Palace of Manufactures

The wall of this building is broken by pilasters and inset decorative panels, and by a series of niches with animal head fountains. The central portal is pure Renaissance architecture, again suggestive of the Roman gateway in form.

The sculptures of the doorway, including the two figures of male and female labor in the niches, and the long high-relief panel, are by Mahonri Young, who is noted for his simple, powerful treatment of modern themes. The panel represents various branches of manufacture, including metal work, blacksmithing, pottery-making, spinning, and architectural sculpture.

Palace of Liberal Arts

The facade here exactly duplicates that just described, even to the niche figures and panel in the portal.

Palace of Education

The Palace of Education has three Renaissance portals on the south facade. These are more Spanish in feeling than those of the two palaces just passed. The tympanum panel of the central doorway may be taken to represent kindergarten teaching, instruction of boys and girls, and self-education in young manhood. It is by Gustave Gerlach. The two panels in the walls over the minor doorways treat very obviously of educational subjects. They are flat in more senses than one, lacking the life of the central tympanum group. They are by students of two American art schools.

The west facade of the Palace of Education is dominated by an immense half-dome, impressive in size and attractively decorated. The style of architecture here is mainly Roman, to harmonize with the Fine Arts Palace which it faces across the lagoon. There are two splendid architectural fountains, under the half-dome here and under, that of the Palace of Food Products.

Sculpture. Flanking the great arch are columns carrying the nude figure of a man, with hands crossed, gazing fixedly in thought. In the official list this is called "Philosophy" or "Thought," and from it the immense portal is called "The Half-dome of Philosophy." But the same figure occupies the corresponding position before the Food Products Palace, and is there called "Physical Vigor." The truth is that the artist designed the statue to suggest that finest of all unions of strength, the physically powerful man thinking. Thus the figure is appropriate to both a food products building and an education building. The figure is strong, but is not so convincing or appealing as the same artist's "Man with a Pick," in the Varied Industries portal. Within the half-dome is a repeated figure with a scroll inscribed "Libris," by Albert Weinert.

The six niches in the west wall have two repeated statues by Charles R. Harley, known as "The Triumph of the Field" and "Abundance." They are simply repeated from the Food Products

Palace to the north, where they properly belong, and will be treated in the next chapter in connection with that building.

On the north facade of the Palace of Education are duplicates of the three south portals, with the same sculptured panels.

Palaces Facing the Marina, and the Column of Progress

The walled-city idea, which throws most of the fine architecture into interior courts, is even more severely carried out in the north facades than in the south. The palaces on the Marina, indeed, present a wall unbroken except by the central doorways and the slight corner projections. The small domes at the corners give a Moorish touch, reminiscent of Southern Spain, and the portals are direct adaptations from Spanish masterpieces.

Palace of Mines

The north facade of the Palace of Mines is free from all ornament except the richly decorative central portal. This is worthy of prolonged study, being one of the finest bits of architectural ornament at the Exposition. It is designed very closely after Spanish models, and is of that transitional period of Spanish architecture that came between the Gothic and the Renaissance, when Gothic had been enriched through the influence of Moorish art, and was just beginning to feel the impulse of the Italian Renaissance. Note how rich is every part of the detail; then note how all detail is subordinated to the mass effect of the whole.

The statues in the niches of the portal are by Allen Newman. The central mantled figure is called the "Conquistador," or conqueror. The artist has here portrayed in spirited fashion a fine type of Spanish nobility. The figure in the side niches, with an old-style pistol in his belt and a rope in his hand, is "The Pirate."

The east facade of the Palace of Mines duplicates that of the Varied Industries Palace, and the west facade forms one side of the north Court of Abundance.

Palace of Transportation

Here the one notably artistic feature is the central portal on the north side, which is an exact replica of the Spanish doorway of the Palace of Mines.

The Column of Progress

This monument symbolizes the energy, the unconquerable spirit that is forever pressing forward to overcome new obstacles, which has led to the building of the Canal. The idea of such a monument was conceived by A. Stirling Calder, the architectural design is from the hand of W. Symmes Richardson, the reliefs at the base are by Isidore Konti, and the crowning statue is by Hermon A. MacNeil. The Column of Progress as a whole is among the finest artistic achievements of the Exposition, and more than any other, perhaps, is worthy of perpetuation in permanent materials to commemorate for all time the opening of the Panama Canal and the holding of the Exposition.

Reliefs at base. The high relief frieze on the square base of the column represents mankind heeding the call to achievement. On the south face are allegoric figures calling mankind to the struggle, the two women holding palm branches, the insignia of victory. On the other three faces are shown groups of figures striving forward at the call, pressing on to achievement, some joyously, some laboriously, some stopped altogether in thought. The whole frieze suggests the beginning of progress.

In the spiral that winds about the column certain interpreters have found a symbol of the upward march of human achievement; but as this spiral decoration is found on the Column of Trajan and the Column of Marcus Aurelius, the Roman prototypes of the Column of Progress, there probably is no special significance in its use here.

Supporting the crowning group is a drum with crouching figures of toilers in relief, entitled "The Burden Bearers."

The Adventurous Bowman is the title of the surmounting statue. The heroic Bowman, facing the skies and the seas, and launching his arrow into the unknown, is the symbol of the impulse that leads men to dare all to achieve victory. At the left of the central figure is a man of smaller stature, leaning against the Bowman to give him support. On the other side a woman crouches, looking up as the arrow speeds on its way. The ring-like object in the woman's hand, which is so hard to identify when one views the group from the ground, is a wreath.

There is about the Bowman a remarkable sense of movement, of energy, of pressing forward, no matter what the view point of the spectator. The monument should be seen from as far north as possible, near the corner of the California building, perhaps. From here, from the Esplanade as one approaches from either east or west, and from the Court of the Universe at the rear, the group has the same inspirational quality, the same sense of joyous effort, of courageous striving toward achievement. The placing of the monument where it closes three important vistas is commended for study to those who have in charge the artistic destinies of our cities.

Palace of Agriculture

The north facade of the Palace of Agriculture is bare except for the central portal, which again duplicates that of the Palace of Mines.

Palace of Food Products

The north facade of this palace duplicates that of the Palace of Agriculture. But when one turns the west corner into Administration Avenue, one finds an entirely different atmosphere, where the Spanish architecture has given way to Italian. The dominating feature of the building's west facade is an immense half-dome, officially called "The Half-dome of Physical Vigor." This is an exact replica of the "Half-dome of Philosophy" on the Education Palace.

Sculpture. Before the half-dome here, on columns, are replicas of Ralph Stackpole's statue of the physically vigorous man in thought. Inside the half-dome is a repeated figure of a man with a wreath, by Earl Cummings.

In the niches along the walls are two alternating compositions, "Abundance" and "The Triumph of the Field," by Charles R. Harley. Abundance is typified by a seated woman, with the conventional overflowing cornucopias beside her, as well as a conglomeration of details suggestive of the riches of land and sea. This group certainly belongs to the Food Products building, but it really ought to be inside, with the flowers made of butter and the tower of raisins. The Triumph of the Field shows a man seated, and around him a museum of ancient symbols of agriculture, and of agricultural triumph, such as were once carried in the annual harvest festivals. These two groups are among the most amusing things at the Exposition; but artistically they can hardly be said to count at all.

The Palace of Machinery

The Palace of Machinery, largest of all the structures at the Exposition, terminates the main building axis at the East. It is monumental in proportions, and is well suited to its purpose of housing an immense display of machines.

Architecture

The architecture was evidently inspired by the great baths of ancient Rome, which were similar in style, size, and detail. The scale is so great-this is said to be the largest wooden building in the world-that it is something of an achievement to have made the structure anything but barn like. By the richness of the cornices and the careful spacing of the openings the architect has made it ornamental, and has given it a sort of noble dignity-though one hesitates to compare it with the palaces of the central group.

The most interesting architectural bit in connection with the Palace of Machinery is the entrance vestibule under the three central archways. Standing at either end of the portico one obtains a remarkable impression of spaciousness combined with decorative completeness. The coloring within the high vestibule is particularly pleasing.

Within the building the unconcealed trussing, instead of giving a sense of barrenness and lack of finish, resolves itself into a sort of lace-like decorative scheme, the whole effect being peculiarly ornamental.

The Palace of Machinery was designed by Clarence R. Ward.

Sculpture

The sculpture here consists of the series of four nude male figures on the column drums, and spandrels for the main and minor doorways, and a widely different group, "The Genius of Creation," before the main western portal. All but the latter group represent "Types of Power."

The figures surmounting columns, flanking the three arches of the central doorway, represent "Steam Power," "Invention," "Electricity," and "Imagination."

Steam is symbolized as a man holding a long lever.

Invention is represented as a man holding forth a miniature winged figure at which he gazes steadily.

The figure of Electricity holds jagged lightning, conventional symbol of electricity.

Imagination, primal power back of all machinery design, is represented by a figure with arm thrown back of head, and seemingly with eyes closed.

Considered simply as portrayals of power, these four virile figures are very successful, and they serve well to carry out the sense of immensity and strength that characterizes the entire building. But they are not at all polished or subtle, lacking the refinement that would make them interesting as something besides vigorous types. All four figures are by Haig Patigian. They are repeated in different order on columns before the north and south portals of the building.

The bas-relief friezes about the bases of the vestibule columns are also by Haig Patigian. The winged figure, typifying "Machinery," lends itself to decorative uses better than the purely human type, and the artist has worked in various mechanical symbols quite cleverly. The cardinal principle in sculptural decoration of this sort is that the frieze, like the whole column, must carry an impression of support. It will be noticed that no room has been left above the head or below the feet; and the disposition of the wings and arms further adds to the feeling that the figures are a true structural unit rather than mere ornament stuck on.

The spandrels over the minor arches in the vestibule, again typifying "Machinery," are equally successful in serving an architectural purpose. Mural sculpture, like mural painting, must never be allowed to "make a hole" in the wall. Notice how fully the figures cover the given space, without any background to draw the eye beyond the surface. These spandrels are also by Haig Patigian. The column reliefs and the spandrels are repeated at the minor doorways of the building.

The Genius of Creation, a magnificently conceived group of sculpture, has been placed, rather unfortunately, in front of the main west portal of the Palace of Machinery. It is by Daniel Chester French, who is generally considered the dean of American sculptors. The Genius of Creation is portrayed as a huge winged figure, enthroned over the formless mass of earth, with head bowed and arms outstretched, calling human life into being. At the two sides a man and a woman, fine strong figures both, stand looking forth, the man courageously, the woman a little more timidly. And at the back, as if to signify the mutual dependence of man and woman, the hands seek to touch. A serpent encircles the base of the group, symbolizing wisdom-or as some prefer to interpret it, everlasting life. This serpent is probably not the one that had so much to do with the life of the first couple on earth.

The statue expresses, of course, the orthodox idea of creation, and it is interesting to contrast it with the sculpture of the Court of Abundance, which in general gives expression to the doctrine of evolution. The strong, almost severe, motherly figure is finely religious in feeling. The sculptor himself has commented on the religious tone that runs through much of the Exposition sculpture, remarking especially the prevalence of winged angel-figures. The reader is left to decide how far this has resulted from the fact that the winged form is essentially decorative, and how far from reverence.

Viewed entirely from the aesthetic side, without regard to the symbolism, the Genius of Creation is one of the most satisfying works on the grounds. It is too bad that it was placed before a background of broken spaces, and before a colorful facade that makes it seem pale. But in it is that reposeful strength which characterizes so much of French's work-a sense of completeness, of fullness, that is perhaps the most soul-satisfying quality of great sculpture.

The South Gardens, Festival Hall, and the Palace of Horticulture

If there is one portion of the Exposition building scheme that does not seem to "belong" to the main group of palaces, it is that which lies south of the Avenue of Palms, including the South Gardens, Festival Hall, and the Palace of Horticulture. The relation of the two buildings to the main courts and palaces is clear: Festival Hall terminating the cross axis through the Court of Abundance and the Court of Flowers; the Palace of Horticulture terminating the cross axis through the Court of the Four Seasons and the Court of Palms. But though the organic relationship is apparent, the least discriminating of critics can see that these buildings are of an architectural style not in harmony with the central group of palaces. Both structures lack that fine sense of proportion and that simple and impressive dignity which characterize the architecture of the courts; and both are more or less pretentious and ornate.

The South Gardens

The South Gardens, like the buildings, have a certain magnificence but at the same time lack any distinctive appeal. The three basins with their fountains are imposing, and the individual beds of flowers are gorgeous in their profuse massing of color; but the distances are so great, and the sense of enclosure that means so much to gardens is so far lacking, that the lover of formal gardening will be less satisfied here than at several other places in the grounds.

Sculpture. The sculpture of the South Gardens is all on the three fountains. The immense central group, the Fountain of Energy, already has been described. In the other two basins the Mermaid Fountain is repeated. This is an attractively ornate bit of decorative design, surmounted by the figure of a mermaid with a dolphin. The figure was modeled from designs by Arthur Putnam. It is typical of the fine strength of his work, and at the same time appealing by the grace of its sinuous lines.

Festival Hall

Festival Hall, designed for the many conventions and musical festivals of the Exposition period, is of typically French architecture of the modern school. The building is not unpleasing, but there is little about it to hold the interest. Robert Farquhar was the architect.

Sculpture. All the sculpture on Festival Hall is the work of Sherry E. Fry. The figures are well suited to their purpose, from the slender "Torch-Bearer," surmounting the minor domes, to the heavy reclining figures on the pylons at the main entrance. Most of the statues are too roughly finished to have more than a decorative interest, but the two groups flanking the main stairway are worthy of study. These two "Flower Girls," one on either side, have a beautiful flowing grace. But quite the most appealing things here are the two minor figures before the pedestals on which the Flower Girls stand. Before the one at the north is a captivating boy Pan with a lizard. Half hidden in the shrubbery at the other side is the sitting figure of a girl, attractively immature and charming in line.

Palace of Horticulture

The Palace of Horticulture is characterized by that combination of Eastern and Western architectural motives which is so noticeable throughout the buildings. The dome is Byzantine, while the rest of the building is of Renaissance, or modern, French architecture. The dome considered alone is an almost perfect bit of design, beautifully proportioned and finely simple. The rest of the building is in general over-decorated, the portals especially being heavily loaded down with meaningless ornament. Apologists for the building say that the profuse ornateness rightly suggests the richness of California's horticulture. Perhaps the best view of the dome is from the east end of the Avenue of the Nations, near the Denmark building, because from there one can see it unobstructed, escaping the disturbing effect of the portals and their spires. The Palace of Horticulture was designed by Bakewell and Brown of San Francisco.

Sculpture. All of the sculpture here is purely decorative. The frieze at the base of each spire, consisting of heavy female figures modeled in pairs, is by E. L. Boutier. The ornamental Caryatides of the porches are by John Bateman.

Palace of Fine Arts

The Fine Arts Palace has been more admired, probably, than any other architectural unit at the Exposition. The reasons are not far to seek. The architect has used those classic forms which for ages have been recognized as best suited to monumental structures, and yet he has used them with originality. The building is classically noble, but without classic austerity or coldness. It is at once beautiful in form, rich in decorative detail, and satisfyingly warm in color. Moreover, it has the finest setting of all the Exposition buildings. The bigness of conception, the boldness with which the largest architectural elements have been handled, the perfect arrangement of architecture, planting, and reflecting waters-all these combine to create the most compelling picture on the grounds.

The arrangement of the building is deceptive. As one looks at it across the lagoon, it seems like a single unit, so well does the planting tie it together, though there are really four unconnected structures: the rotunda, two detached peristyles at the sides, and the art gallery proper at the back.

Architecture

The style of architecture is Classic, freely treated. The rotunda is Roman. The peristyle is more Greek in feeling, in the simplicity of general form, with splendidly modeled capitals, full strong columns, and dignified cornice. The curved facade of the main building, facing the rotunda and peristyle, is very original in its arrangement of classic architectural motives and masses of foliage, with a Pompeian pergola on top.

The color scheme of the whole building is worthy of study. And although the structure when seen by day deserves all the praise that has been bestowed upon it, by night its beauty is beyond description. One should sit long at the edge of the lagoon opposite the rotunda, and watch the illuminated building itself and its reflection in the waters below, to feel the full spell of it. No one should miss, either, the walk between the peristyle and the main building on one of those nights when there is soft local illumination, for nowhere else on the grounds has the poetry of lighting been so perfectly realized.

The architect of the Fine Arts Palace was Bernard R. Maybeck, a Californian.

Sculpture

The sculpture about the lagoon, including that under the peristyle and rotunda, is to be treated in the next chapter, except that which is definitely a part of the building's integral decorative scheme.

The reliefs outside the rotunda, on the attic above the cornice, represent man's effort to gain the ideal of art. To see these reliefs best, one should stand directly across the lagoon from the rotunda. In the panel facing East one sees the figure of Art personified. On either side is a group showing the champions of art combating centaurs, that stand for the commonplace, materialistic things of life. In the next panel to the left, facing Southeast, is represented the bridling of the winged horse Pegasus, which to the Greeks symbolized the attainment of poetic inspiration. Here also are figures representing the arts of literature, sculpture and music, by the familiar symbols, a lamp, a statuette and a lute. The panel to the right of the center one shows Apollo, sun-god and patron-god of the arts, drawn in his chariot, with a procession of devotees. These panels are repeated on the other five faces about the dome. They are among the finest reliefs on the Exposition buildings, and are by Bruno Louis Zimm.

The figures within the rotunda, surmounting the eight columns are "Priestesses of Culture," by Herbert Adams.

The flower-box sculptures are by Ulric H. Ellerhusen-both those on the ground and those at the corners of the boxes surmounting the peristyle. The ladies on the latter, looking so steadily into the boxes, do not represent "Curiosity." The plan was to have masses of foliage overflowing, and half-covering the figures; and when this was given up, the decorative women gave the unexpected impression of being deeply absorbed in something happening out of sight of the spectator below. An explanation which has gained some currency is that the figures represent "Introspection," which seems quite apropos.

The kneeling figure (unnamed) on the edge of the lagoon before the rotunda is by Ralph Stackpole. It is one of the most appealing bits of all the Exposition sculpture, well expressing devotion and reverence. It cannot be reached from the rotunda side, this portion of the shore being closed to the public.

The figure over the doorway of the gallery is Leo Lentelli's "Aspiration." During the early months of the Exposition this statue was suspended from behind, the base on which it now stands having been placed late in the Spring. As the figure first appeared, hanging in air, it caused more comment than any other sculpture on the grounds. The most appropriate explanation was that since the figure lacked any visible means of support it probably was meant to represent "California Art." Even the recent alterations have failed to save it from seeming graceless and out of place.

Mural Paintings

The eight panels in the dome of the rotunda are by Robert Reid. There are two series of four paintings each, called "The Birth and Influence of Art," and "The Four Gold's of California." They form perhaps the least interesting of the several groups of murals, being vague in meaning, unpleasantly restless in composition, and only occasionally attractive in coloring.

The easiest panel to identify is that called "The Birth of Oriental Art," which is on the west wall, closest to the doorway of the main building. Starting with this and following around the dome to the right, the pictures are in this order:

1. The Birth of Oriental Art. A man in armor on a fanciful, dragon is attacking an eagle, symbolizing man's effort to attain the inspiration of the heavens. Below, China can be recognized in the man with a brilliant colored robe, and Japan in the woman with the bright parasol.

2. Gold is symbolized by a woman with a wand, on a cornucopia overflowing with gold.

3. The Ideals of All Art. The ideals which animate artists are shown: Truth with her glass; Religion typified in the Madonna and child; Beauty, with the peacock; and the Militant Ideal with a flag. Above and below are figures carrying the wreath and the palm, the artist's tokens of success in attaining the ideal.

4. Poppies, the second "gold" of California.

5. The Birth of European Art. Four figures surround an altar on which burns the sacred fire, three being merely attendants preserving the flame, and the fourth the guardian holding high a torch lit at the altar. A man from earth grasps this torch as he leans from his flying chariot. A woman in the lower corner holds a crystal gazing-globe, wherein the future of art has been revealed, and she turns to gaze after the man who is carrying the sacred fire to earth.

6. Citrus Fruits, the third "gold" of California.

7. The Inspiration of All Art. Two Angels of Inspiration are at the top, while below to the left are Sculpture, with a winged statuette, and Architecture, with the scroll and compass; and to the right, Painting, with brush and palette, Music, with a lyre, and Poetry, with a book.

8. Wheat, the fourth "gold" of California.

The Outdoor Gallery of Sculpture

Many of the finest bronzes and marbles of the sculpture section are given an adequate setting which would be impossible within the gallery building, by being placed in the open, along the two ends of the lagoon, through the peristyles, and under the Fine Arts rotunda.

As this group of sculpture embraces all types from the playful to the very serious, it is foolish to try to appreciate the whole series at one time. Perhaps the best way is to start first to familiarize oneself with the smaller bronzes of the purely lyric type, the charming garden figures, sun-dials, and miniature fountains, that make up such an attractive part of the collection. Note how often the names of Edward Berge, Janet Scudder and Anna Coleman Ladd recur in connection with this graceful, intimately appealing sort of sculpture. On another day, when life seems soberer, spend all your time in study of the more serious works, such as Saint Gaudens' "Seated Lincoln," and McKenzie's "The Young Franklin," noting how the dignity, sureness of touch, and sound purpose of these make them more appealing with longer acquaintance. On another day take the intermediate group, that is dignified but less austere in theme-such works as Sherry Fry's "Peace," and Berge's "Muse Finding the Head of Orpheus." Studied systematically, there is in this series of statues a broad education in the appreciation of sculpture.

For convenience in reference the whole series is listed here. In regard to those works which the labels make self-explanatory, no comment is added, unless to call attention to some special quality which the unpracticed eye might miss. Where the symbolism or "story" is obscure, an explanation is given.

South of the lagoon are: 1. Sea Lions by Frederick G. R. Roth. 2. The Scout by Cyrus E. Dallin. Note the remarkable clean-cut quality of this equestrian statue. 3. Wind and Spray fountain, by Anna Coleman Ladd. 4. Diana by Haig Patigian-a graceful statue of the Greek goddess of the hunt, which is in marked contrast to the same artist's strong figures on the Palace of Machinery. 5. Peace by Sherry E. Fry. This beautifully modeled figure has a classic simplicity that is worthy of study. 6. American Bison by A. P. Proctor.

Beyond the second Bison, beside the roadway that runs behind the Fine
Arts Palace, is a model of the Kirkpatrick Monument, at Syracuse, New
York, by Gail Sherman Corbett. The central figures represent an Indian
discovering to a Jesuit priest the waters of an historic salt spring at Syracuse.

In the circle at the south end of the peristyle are: 1. Seated Lincoln by Augustus St. Gaudens generally considered one of the noblest works of the greatest American sculptor. Note especially the dignity of the whole, and the sympathetic modeling of the face. 2. Bust of Halsey C. Ives by Victor S. Holm. 3. Bust of William Howard Taft by Robert Aitken. 4. Henry Ward Beecher by John Quincy Adams Ward-a dignified and well-known life-size statue.

Along the south peristyle are (at the right) 1. Piping Pan by Louis St. Gaudens. 2. Flying Cupid by Janet Scudder. 3. Muse Finding the Head of Orpheus by Edward Berge-a marble well expressive of gentle grief. Orpheus, sweetest musician of Greek mythology, after failing to recover his beloved Eurydice from the underworld, in his sorrow scorned the Thracian nymphs, who in their anger dismembered him. His head was washed up by the sea and found by the sorrowing Muses. 4. (At the left) Michael Angelo by Robert Aitken, showing the master-sculpture at work on one of his famous figures. 5. (At the right) Young Pan by Janet Scudder. 6. (At the left) Wood Nymph by Isidore Konti. 7. Young Mother with Child by Furio Piccirilli. 8. (At the right) Wild Flower by Edward Berge. 9. (At the left) Eurydice by Furio Piccirilli. 10. (At the right) Boy and Frog by Edward Berge. 11. (At the left) Dancing Nymphs by Olin L. Warner. 12. Idyl by Olga Popoff Muller. 13. An Outcast by Attilio Piccirilli. 14. (Beside the doorway) Youth by Charles Carey Rumsey. Before the doorway is to be placed The Pioneer Mother Monument by Charles Grafly.

About the rotunda are: 1. (Outside the southwest archway) Thomas Jefferson by Karl Bitter. 2. (In center of rotunda) Lafayette by Paul Wayland Bartlett-the statue given by America to France. 3. Lincoln by Daniel Chester French, a dignified portrayal that cannot be justly judged from the plaster model here exhibited. 4. Relief by Richard H. Recchia, representing "Architecture." 5. Commodore Barry Memorial by John J. Boyle. 6. Relief by Richard H. Recchia, representing "Architecture." 7. Princeton Student Memorial by Daniel Chester French a noble treatment of a difficult theme. 8. The Young Franklin by Robert Tait McKenzie. This is a fine conception, in which the sculptor has escaped from the conventional path of monumental portraiture. 9. (On walls of west archway) Reliefs by Bela L. Pratt, representing "Sculpture." 10. (Outside west archway) Portrait of a Boy by Albin Polasek. 11. The Awakening by Lindsey Morris Sterling. 12. (Beside northwest archway) William Cullen Bryant by Herbert Adams.

Along the north peristyle are: 1. (Beside main doorway of gallery) Beyond by Chester Beach. 2. The Sower by Albin Polasek. 3. The Centaur by Olga Popoff Muller. 4. Boy with Fish by Bela L. Pratt. 5. (At the right) Returning from the Hunt by John J. Boyle. 6. (At the left) L'Amour by Evelyn Beatrice Longman-a marble wherein the woman's figure is tenderly beautiful. 7. Garden Figure by Edith Woodman Burroughs. 8. (At the right) Fighting Boys Fountain by Janet Scudder. 9. Soldier of Marathon by Paul Noquet. 10. (At the left) Youth by Victor D. Salvatore. 11. (At the right) Primitive Man by Olga Popoff Muller. 12. The Scalp by Edward Berge-an unpleasant bit of realism. 13. (At the left) Apollo by Haig Patigian. 14. (At the right) A Faun's Toilet by Attilio Piccirilli. 15. Duck Baby Fountain by Edith Barretto Parsons. 16. Maiden of the Roman Campagna by Albin Polasek-a figure instinct with the spirit of the antique.

On the circle at the north end of the peristyle are: 1. (At the right) Young Diana by Janet Scudder-a young goddess of the hunt, conceived in modern spirit, with remarkable freedom and grace of movement. 2. Great Danes by Anna Vaughan Hyatt. 3. (In walk) Sundial by Harriet W. Frishmuth. 4. Bondage by Carl Augustus Heber. 5. Boy Pan with Frog by Clement J. Barnhorn. 6. Sundial by Gail Sherman Corbett. 7. Three fountain groups in one basin, all by Anna Coleman Ladd. Of these the Sun God and Python has been especially admired as a spirited and graceful bit of work. 8. (On the lagoon side of the circle) Mother of the Dead by C. S. Pietro-a sincere and powerfully realistic work, and quite unlike anything else in the outdoor gallery. 9. (In walk) Chief Justice Marshall by Herbert Adams. 10. Destiny by C. Percival Dietsch. 11. Sundial by Edward Berge. 12: Daughter of Pan by R. Hinton Perry. 13. Head of Lincoln by Adolph A. Weinman.

Along the roadway to the left, as one leaves the circle, are two sculptures: Bird Fountain by Caroline Risque, and Prima Mater by Victor S. Holm.

North of the lagoon are: 1. Fragment of the Fountain of Time by Lorado
Taft. 2. Nymph by Edmond T. Quinn. 3. Dying Lion by Paul Wayland
Bartlett. 4. Rock and Flower Group by Anna Coleman Ladd. 5. Whale-man by
Bela L. Pratt.

On the island at the north end of the lagoon is a fountain by Robert Paine.

The Fine Arts Galleries

Do not visit the Fine Arts exhibits blindly, without knowing what they are aimed to show; and do not try to see the whole exhibition in one day. First understand the scope and arrangement of the displays, and then follow some definite system by which you are sure to get the best out of each individual section. It is better to see one part thoroughly than to carry away a confused impression of the whole.

The scope of the exhibit is limited to painting, sculpture and print-making, except in the Oriental sections. In painting the primary aim has been to make a representative display of contemporary work. Most of the galleries contain only canvases painted within the last ten years. But in order to correct the common misconception that American art is entirely a thing of today, without historical background, a few rooms are given up to historic works of the various early American schools, and to works of the foreign schools that have influenced the development of American art.

The arrangement of the galleries should be mastered before one starts to study. In general there are three divisions of exhibits. At each end is a group of foreign sections, and the great middle space is given up to American art. The accompanying diagram is designed primarily to make clear the location of the several divisions. The visitor will find it worth while to remember that a main central corridor runs the whole length of the United States Section. By continually referring to this corridor, one can keep one's bearings fairly well.

The method of seeing the galleries that is suggested in this guide is based on the official classification as far as possible: the foreign sections are taken in order, and the historical section is treated in that chronological sequence which the directors intended to show forth. But there is no system in the arrangement of the twenty-eight general rooms of contemporary American work, In treating these the guide aims to suggest tendencies and influences, rather than to point out this or that canvas as a good or bad one. Nevertheless it is believed that every really important picture or artist is individually mentioned-so that one who has used the manual consistently may be sure of having enjoyed the cream of the collection, at the same time gaining the wider knowledge of the main currents of development.

It is necessary to use to a certain extent the arbitrary subject-divisions, such as portrait, landscape, and figure painting; and to refer also to realistic painting, which tends to depict things as they are, as opposed to the academic, which recognizes the wisdom of conventionalization or idealization. But the most important distinction, for the student of contemporary tendencies, is that which concerns the term "Impressionism." This name in its original and technical sense applied to the works of the men who, instead of mixing shades, placed different colors side by side on their canvases to give the effect of the right shade at a distance. As the experiments of these artists were directed chiefly to the solution of problems of light, the term naturally was widened to include that whole division of painting which is concerned with atmospheric aspects and color harmonies rather than with subject-interest and line composition. Terms which express the same idea in general or in part, are "luminism" and "plein-air painting." Impressionism has had more effect on the current of art than has any other movement in history. Not only in the handling of light and in freshness of coloring has the whole of painting been profoundly changed, but there is a general tendency to paint the impression rather than the actuality, the harmonious effect rather than the literal fact-and these things are notably illustrated in the Exposition galleries.

For the sake of the visitor who comes to the gallery with practically no knowledge of art, a word may profitably be said about critical standards. First remember that there are many qualities which may make a painting worth while: pleasing design, beautiful color, a compelling expression of emotion or thought, or a poetic suggestion of a fleeting aspect or mood. It is necessary to judge each particular work by the artist's intention, and not by untrained personal tastes. Before passing judgment learn to know the picture well. You may find that you have been attracted by something superficial. On the other hand, you may find that the seemingly less attractive picture, which has been recommended by people of trained judgment, grows more and more pleasing with riper acquaintance. Go slowly, study thoroughly what you study, and keep an open mind-for that way leads to the widest enjoyment.

United States Section: Painting

The United States Section consists chiefly of contemporary work, but includes a small historical section, which is to be found to the left as one enters at the main doorway. It is in this part of the exhibit that one should start.

The Historical Section consists of two well-defined parts. The first contains examples of foreign schools of painting that have influenced American art. The second contains the works of American painters from the beginnings to the early Twentieth Century. The Foreign Historical Section occupies rooms 91-92 and 61-63.

Gallery 91-Early Schools. A gallery of old paintings, chiefly of the Italian, Flemish and Dutch Schools, designed to suggest the earliest roots of American art. Practically all the canvases are mere echoes of the "old masters," and they may well be passed over hastily by all but the most thorough historical student.

Gallery 92-French Influence. This gallery and the next two are designed to show works of those schools, chiefly French, that have had direct influence upon American art. On wall A is a painting by Courbet, interesting in the light of that artist's influence on Whistler's early work. But most important here are the examples of the Barbizon School, romantic landscape painters of the mid-Nineteenth Century, who had much to do with the development of the Inness-Wyant group in America. On wall B are two canvases by Corot, both badly placed, one of which (1486) is typically poetic and beautiful. The examples by Daubigny and Rousseau on wall C are not satisfying. On wall D the two Monticellis suggest the source of some of the rich qualities of the work of Keith and similar American painters.

Gallery 62, adjoining 92, shows the best example of Barbizon work, in Troyon's beautiful "Landscape and Cattle" on wall C. On wall A is a small painting, interesting but not characteristic, by Millet, who influenced the whole world of art toward sincerity. On wall B is Sir Laurens Alma-Tadema's "Among the Ruins," sole representative here of the English School of "polished" painters that strongly influenced a number of American artists. On wall D are two very interesting portrait studies by Franz von Lenbach, intended to suggest the influence of the Munich School on American art, before Americans began to flock to Paris to study.

Gallery 61-Recent French Influence. On wall A is an uneven collection by Monet, the greatest apostle of Impressionism. This group, with the exception perhaps of the sea-shore scene, should be studied thoroughly, in regard to the technique that juxtaposes colors to give the right resultant tone at a distance; in regard to the general tendency to subordinate subject interest to the expression of fleeting aspects; and in regard to the masterly handling of light. No other group will be referred to so often in connection with the American galleries. On wall B is a typically joyous canvas by Gaston La Touche, who carries Impressionism into figure work. On walls C and D are other examples of the Impressionist School, by Pissarro and Renoir and the English Sisley. On wall C is a portrait by Eugene Carriere. On wall D is a panel by Puvis de Chavannes, who has influenced modern mural painting more than any other artist. This picture has the typical union of the classic feeling with very modern technique, but it is representative of de Chavannes' manner rather than of his whole art at its best.

Gallery 63-English Influence. This is the richest of the historical rooms. Although there is a scattered collection including the names of Van Dyke, Guido Reni, Tiepolo, Ribera, Velasquez, Goya, and Turner, on walls A and B, the important thing is the fine collection of the English portraitists. Here are examples, many of them among the finest, by Hogarth, Reynolds, Gainsborough, Romney, Lawrence, and Hoppner. It is hardly necessary to point out the close connection between the work of this English group and early American painting, since a visit to the adjoining gallery 60 will show how the first important development in the States grew out of the art of the mother country.

The American Historical Section covers the entire development of American painting from the beginning to the early years of the present century. To obtain the proper sequence, one should start in room 60, working gradually down to 57, then visiting 64 and 54.

Gallery 60 contains a profusion of fine examples of the early portrait school, which was so closely connected with English art of the time. Gilbert Stuart, the most important figure, is represented by an extensive collection on wall A. In this room, too, are canvases by West, Peale, Copley, and their followers well into the Nineteenth Century.

Gallery 59 contains chiefly the work of that barren mid-century period when portraiture and landscape painting alike became hard and labored. Insofar as any foreign influences can be detected here, they are of the "tight" schools of England and Germany.

Gallery 58 contains some interesting work of the latter half of the Nineteenth Century-notably the paintings by Eastman Johnson, an important figure of the time when American art was finding itself. Albert Bierstadt's two landscapes are typical of the so-called Hudson River School, the mechanical forerunner of the Inness-Wyant group. An interesting contrast is offered here by H. J. Breuer's "Santa Inez Mountains," a contemporary landscape that is full of the freshness and light of present-day American painting.

Gallery 57 shows another great step in advance. A generous portion of the space is given to Edwin A. Abbey, an American-born artist who really was more a part of English art. The exhibit shows clearly that Abbey was greater as illustrator than as painter, the finest things here being the exquisite pen drawings. Wall D has five paintings by John LaFarge, who by his work and by his theories greatly influenced American art at the end of the century. Worthy of study, too, are the more modern landscapes of Theodore Robinson.

From this room one should turn back into the central line of galleries.

Gallery 64 contains historical American paintings that range through the latter half of the last century and into this, with such well-known names as Parrish, Gifford, Hunt, Wylie, Martin, the Morans, Eakins, and even the more recent Frederic Remington.

Such pictures as F. E. Church's "Niagara Falls" (wall A), J. G. Brown's "The Detective Story" (wall B), and Thomas Hovenden's "Breaking Home Ties" (wall D), are typical of what was accepted as the best work a generation or two ago.

Passing through room 65, one should next go to 54.

Gallery 54 is the most important in the American Historical Section, for it shows the work of the men who really emancipated American painting from the old hardness and tightness of technique, and from the old sentimentalism. Wall A is given up to the work of the late Winslow Homer, who has been called "the most American of painters." The seashore scenes alone of the things here are representative of this big man at his best. Wall B has a varied assortment by lesser painters, but ones of importance: Blakelock, Currier, William Morris Hunt, and Fuller. On walls C and D the very important canvases are those by Inness and Wyant, men who were deeply influenced by the French Barbizon School, but whose individual achievement marked the first great stride toward the bigness, freedom and lightness of present-day American landscape painting.

Contemporary American Painting. Leaving aside the one-man rooms for the present, it is just as well to turn from the last historical room, 54, into 55, and progress in natural order through 56, 65, 85, 66 (the central hall), and 80. The contemporary rooms north of the central hall can be best visited in three groups, each following the official room numbering: first, 67 to 74; then 43 to 51; and finally the detached section at the far north end of the building, 117 to 120.

Gallery 55 has a well assorted collection of contemporary canvases, but includes no outstanding features.

Gallery 56 is a typical modern American room, with good landscapes in the work of Breuer, Borg, Davol, and Stokes.

Gallery 65 contains some of the best American figure paintings in the building. The finest group is that by Cecilia Beaux on wall D, which well displays that remarkable artist's brilliant technique and "flair." It is notable how many of the really virile paintings here are by women -many of them of the younger groups. From Marion Pooke's polished but free "Silhouettes," and Alice Kent Stoddard's appealing "Sisters," to M. Jean McLane's joyously brilliant canvases on wall C, there is a wide range of achievement and promise.

Gallery 85. On walls A and B are five canvases by Horatio Walker that are worthy of attention. But finer are Charles W. Hawthorne's four paintings on walls B and D. Their bigness of conception, sincerity and soundness of technique mark a coming master. Wall C is given up to a display by Charles Walter Stetson, which shows, more strongly than any other in the American section, that tendency to the decorative and the idyllic which is to be noted as so strong in recent painting. On wall D are three works of George deForest Brush, a man who has been but little influenced by the more radical tendencies. "The Potter" is interesting for the painstaking and minute finish of varying surface textures.

Gallery 66-Central Hall. Although the important places here are given to sculpture, there are a few very interesting paintings: some representative landscapes, and at the ends decorative panels by Alexander Harrison and by Howard Cushing.

Gallery 80 is notable for the work of painters who have followed rather closely the old academic traditions: for the smooth and polished canvases of W. M. Paxton and Philip Leslie Hale. There are also seven landscapes by Willard L. Metcalf, fresh attractive work of the "plein-air" school.

Gallery 67 is rich in fine landscapes, and contains the best of the exhibition's marines. Here are the only works of Charles H. Davis, a notable follower of the poetic Inness School, and of Leonard Ochtman and Ben Foster, who stand well to the fore among the more vigorous landscapists. Also worthy of attention are the landscapes of Braun, Borg, White, Wendt, J. F. Carlson, Rosen and Browne. The marines represent well a department of painting in which Americans have long excelled; on wall A are four by Paul Dougherty, on B and C three by Frederick J. Waugh, and on D one by Emil Carlsen. Of the other paintings the most interesting is the idyllic bit by Hugo Ballin on wall C, representative of the decorative tendency.

Gallery 68 contains as its most important exhibit three portraits by J. C. Johansen, on wall B, all typical of the brilliant fluency of this remarkable painter. Among the landscapes here the most important are the two Schofields on wall D, typical of the best and sanest phase of Impressionism in America. Very important too are the canvases by Daniel Garber on wall C.

Gallery 69 contains a mixed collection, with such different good things as Lawton Parker's polished figure studies (wall B) and J. Francis Murphy's poetic landscape (wall C). On wall C is a painting by John W. Alexander, one of the leaders in American art, which is typical of his method of subordinating subject interest to line arrangement and color composition.

Gallery 70-Portrait Room. On wall C are three portraits by Irving R. Wiles, and on D two by Julian Story-both names long well-known in American art. But the surprising thing is that several of the canvases by less known men stand up with, or even surpass, these.

Gallery 71 is notable chiefly for some good landscapes.

Gallery 72 contains little to hold the attention, unless it is the group of canvases by Walter McEwen, who shows adherence to the older traditions, not only in smoothness of technique, but in sentimentalism and general prettiness.

Gallery 73 is given up chiefly to Alson Clark's over-sketchy and intemperately colored Panama pictures. The most interesting thing here is Ernest Lawson's "Beginning of Winter," on wall B, a representative work by one of the most successful American followers of Impressionism.

Gallery 74 is a room of good landscapes, with a few outstanding canvases like Will S. Robinson's "Group of White Birches" on wall C.

A new start should be made here by passing through rooms 70 and 71 to 43, from which the numerical order can be followed back to room 51, adjoining the central hall.

Galleries 43 and 44 have a range from many mediocre to a few really good things, lacking anything that demands special attention.

Gallery 45 is a room rich in comparative values. Note the delicacy of treatment and of color in William Sartain's three landscapes, on wall A, and in Birge Harrison's atmospheric paintings on wall D. Compare these with the heavily painted and richly colored canvases by Walter Griffin on wall C, and then with the more straightforward, vigorous work of Charles Morris Young on wall B. Harrison, Griffin and Young, at least, are of the distinctly modern school; but note how individually each has utilized his inheritance of vibrating color and light. On wall A are two fine figure studies by Robert Reid, an innovator and a really great painter, though he did not show it when he painted the panels for the Fine Arts rotunda.

Gallery 46. There is much poor material here; but on walls B and C are some paintings by Frank Vincent Dumond that are interesting for their fresh coloring and their solving of light problems.

Gallery 47 contains evidences of progress in varied lines, from E. L. Blumenschein's big Indian pictures, and Cohn Campbell Cooper's studies of American cities, to the experiment in painting flesh against a richly varied background, by Richard Miller, a gifted American who has long lived in Paris.

Gallery 48 contains much promising work of various tendencies, but no outstanding features.

Gallery 49 contains, on wall A, a splendid collection of the work of Dwight W. Tryon, one of the older school of landscapists, who helped to break the way for the moderns and has kept up with them to a great extent. With the exception of one canvas, the pictures on walls B and D are by J. Alden Weir, another roadbreaker, and an experimenter with new effects of light and atmosphere. In such canvases as "June" and "White Oak" one finds some of the best that American art has built on the theories of Monet.

Gallery 50 contains some good landscapes, but nothing that demands special attention aside from Sergeant Kendall's refined figure studies.

Gallery 51 is given over in general to the independents and extremists of American art. Here are canvases by Glackens, Sloan, and Breckenridge, rather disappointing to one who has watched hopefully the movement they represent. Certainly their exhibits are suggestive of a rather undisciplined vigor and freedom. On wall C the five canvases in the lower row are by Robert Henri. They are the experiments of a master, rather than his best works. The truly representative Henri picture is the "Lady in Black Velvet," on wall D. This has a wonderful synthetic quality, a suppression of detail and a spotting of interest at the important point. There is, too, a spiritual quality that is lacking in the other canvases. On the other side of the doorway is Gertrude Lambert's "Black and Green," a notably fine canvas.

The only other general rooms of the contemporary American section are those at the far north end of the building, beyond the foreign sections, numbered from 117 to 120.

Gallery 117 is a sort of catch-all room, in which are many things that never should have been admitted to the galleries. The really interesting feature is the series of canvases by Frieseke, full of light and freedom. Gallery 118 is less mediocre on the whole, but lacks any features of special appeal. Gallery 119 includes a surprising conglomeration of paintings and drawings in all mediums, wherein the extremists have their say. There is a wealth of interest here, but one must have time to separate the bad from the good. Gallery 120 is also marked generously by the newer tendencies. The important feature is the group of virile paintings by George Bellows, on wall C. These mark the most successful American attempt to grasp sanely the bigness and freedom of the post-Impressionist movements.

One-man Rooms. As a part of the plan to show the various influences on the course of American art, it was decided to give up a number of rooms to individual displays by leaders of the several well-marked tendencies. Galleries 75-79, 87-90, and 93, at the east side of the building on either side of the center, contain these "one-man shows."

Gallery 75-Sargent. Here are shown a number of canvases by the man generally considered the greatest living American painter-certainly the greatest of the portraitists. Though containing none of the really famous paintings, there are portraits which show the typical Sargent brilliancy-the swift sureness and the perfect balance of restraint and freedom. The James portrait is especially worthy of study.

Gallery 76-Mathews. In this room are shown a number of canvases by Arthur F. Mathews, most important of the California painters, as well as a few by Francis MacComas, another Californian. Mathews stands primarily for the decorative tendency. His canvases have a noble sense of repose that is too often lacking in contemporary work, and there is remarkable color harmony here.

Gallery 77-Melchers. Here are representative works by Gari Melchers, a famous American who has long lived abroad. Unmistakably these canvases are from a masterly brush; but the coloring is not always good, and the room is somewhat disappointing.

Gallery 78-Hassam. By common consent Childe Hassam is considered the greatest American follower of Impressionism. He is an innovator who has carved a sure place for himself by adding a new vigor to the methods of the original Impressionists. Such decorative canvases as 2033 on wall B, and such delicate ones as 2029 on wall D, should be compared with the Monets in room 61.

Gallery 79-Chase. This room is designed to show the work of an American who was greatly influenced by the Munich School of painters. William M. Chase, both in his portraits and in his remarkable still-life studies, shows the fine German thoroughness rather than French brilliancy. The four canvases that hold the places of honor on all four walls show clearly the influence of Whistler.

Gallery 87-Duveneck. Here are works by Frank Duveneck, who like Chase studied at Munich. Sound in draughtsmanship, steady, and well-thought out, they maintain a remarkable standard of excellence. It is instructive to step from here into the adjoining large gallery, where the French influence is predominant.

Gallery 88-Redfield. In the winter scenes of E. W. Redfield one finds the sure touch of a master of the new and vigorous school of American landscapists. Redfield has modified Impressionism, clinging to a certain reality, and yet achieving the sparkling atmospheric effects of the luminists.

Gallery 89-Tarbell. In contrast to Hassam and Redfield and Twachtman is Edmund C. Tarbell, who has taken but little from the Impressionist group. His most characteristic and most appealing work can be seen in the canvases on wall A, beautifully lighted interiors which show the academic tendency, but in a new and delightful way.

Gallery 90-Keith. This collection of canvases, with its sameness of subject and arrangement, is hardly typical of the late William Keith at his best. He was the western representative of the Inness-Wyant school of the late Nineteenth Century, though he leaned more to the romantic than did the others.

Gallery 93-Twachtman. Here are the works of a painter who is closer to Monet than to the more vigorous American school of modified Impressionism. It is well to study one wall, A perhaps, and then to go to the Redfield and Hassam rooms, and then to the group of Monets, to see the various ways in which Impressionism has spread.

Gallery 26-Whistler. The Whistler room is quite appropriately placed with the foreign historical rooms, rather than with the other one-man galleries-as if Whistler should be grouped with the influences rather than the influenced. The room contains none of the artist's finest paintings, but is well representative of the several sides of his work. Wall D shows Whistler the portraitist, with "his faces and figures that emerge from a soft black background, very much as one sees a person in the gathering twilight." On walls A and B it is Whistler the colorist, and on wall B especially, Whistler the rediscoverer of Japanese color and figure composition. On wall D is the "Study of Jo," an uncharacteristic early work, which shows the influence of Courbet.

American Section: Prints

The American prints occupy rooms 29 to 34, along the west wall of the building just south of the central vestibule. The exhibit is very representative, and contains both historical and contemporary sections.

Gallery 29-Prints by Whistler. Here is a collection of Whistler's etchings and lithographs, with a few drawings. The distinguishing quality is an exquisite delicacy.

Gallery 30-Historical Prints. In this room one can trace the development of American engraving and etching from the beginnings to the present day. Starting on wall D one finds steel engraving illustrated from the days of Paul Revere to its decadence; then the history of wood-engraving to its flowering in Cole and Wolf; early and recent American etching; and a few modern copper engravings and lithographs.

Gallery 31-Prints by Pennell. This room contains a splendid collection of prints from all of Joseph Pennell's important series, in etching, lithography and mezzotint-a remarkable display by one of the world's greatest etchers.

Galleries 32 and 33-Contemporary Etchers. These two rooms contain a rich collection of contemporary American work that should be studied print by print. Even a superficial look will indicate that even without Pennell and Whistler the American etchers are doing work universally worth while.

Gallery 34-Color Prints. Here is an interesting collection of color prints in both etching and wood engraving. It shows the achievement of the younger artists in mediums that were practically unknown in this country ten years ago.

American Section: Illustration

Galleries 41 and 42 are given up to drawings and paintings by Howard
Pyle, who has been called "the father of modern American illustration."

Gallery 26, adjoining the Italian section, contains a small but fairly interesting group of original drawings for illustration. In the work of Wyeth, Schoonover, Elizabeth Shippen Green, Jessie Wilcox Smith, and others, there is very strong evidence of Howard Pyle's influence. On wall B of this room, and in the adjoining gallery 27, there is a collection of photographs of American sculpture and mural paintings.

Gallery 36, adjoining the main west vestibule, has a miscellaneous collection of drawings and paintings in all mediums, ranging from the most delicate and polished to caricature and sketchiness run riot. There is a great deal of interest, but little that is important in a big way.

American Section: Miniatures

Galleries 37 and 40 contain an excellent collection of miniatures, ranging from a work by Malbone, the first important American in this field, to that of such notable contemporaries as W. J. Baer, Laura C. Hills, and Lucia Fairchild Fuller.

In both miniature rooms there are a number of paintings and drawings, in various mediums, including, in room 40, a few oils by Jules Guerin, the color wizard of the Exposition.

American Section: Sculpture

Of the monumental sculpture of the American Section most of the finest examples are out-of-doors. The central hall of the gallery building contains a collection that is worth studying piece by piece, including such notable things as Daniel Chester French's "Alice Freeman Palmer Memorial," Karl Bitter's "Signing the Louisiana Purchase Treaty" and "Tappan Memorial," and Robert Aitken's "Mausoleum Door."

But by far the most notable thing about the sculpture display is the extensive collection of charming small bronzes, which is scattered through the many rooms. The visitor should especially make sure of seeing certain individual group exhibits, such as the very freely rendered figures by Paul Troubetzkoy in the International Room (108), Paul Manship's groups, with their touch of classic appeal, in gallery 93, and the cases of statuettes by Abastenia St. Leger Eberle and Bessie Potter Vonnoh, in gallery 65. Very rich in interest, too, is the collection of medals and plaques, shown in galleries 38 and 39.

Foreign Sections

The foreign sections are in two groups, at the two ends of the building. There is no system in their arrangement, and they are treated here in the order in which they happen to be placed, beginning at the far south end.

The Japanese Section occupies galleries 1 to 10. To appreciate Japanese art it is necessary to become accustomed to the conventionalization of treatment-to understand what the artist was after, and to judge from that standpoint. It is well to begin by studying works that are more like Western art-such things as "Moving Clouds" (15) and "Evening: Nawa Harbor" (12) in room 1-and then to progress to the works in which the conventions are more pronounced. Note, throughout the paintings in rooms 1, 2 and 3, the delicacy of tone, the color harmony, and the fine sense of composition and pattern.

In galleries 8 and 10 are collections of Japanese sculpture and painting, done in the Western manner. It is interesting to see what the Oriental artist can accomplish in an alien medium; but neither for the Japanese nor for the American can these works have the same genuine appeal as those in galleries 1 to 3. The other rooms contain a varied collection of porcelain, embroidery, wood and ivory carving, and prints.

The French Section is one of the most interesting, but is hardly representative of the best that country has achieved in art. The general average is such that it upholds France's traditional standing as the home of "good painting," but this is by no means a collection of masterpieces. The most noticeable tendency is that toward the decorative. The galleries of the French section have been re-numbered, beginning with 1.

Gallery 1 is a rather poor room on the whole, though it, contains two canvases on the north wall by Lucien Simon, typical of that artist's masterly breadth of treatment. On the west wall, beside the doorway, are two of Aman-Jean's portraits. The little landscape (429) under one of these, by Marcel-Clement, is notable, as are also Jean Domerque's decorative canvas on the south wall and Maury's three nude girls on the north.

Gallery 2 is most interesting for the group on the north wall, where the place of honor is given to Henri Martin's work. Here is an artist who has carried Impressionism to its limit of vibrating light and color. The large central canvas should be seen from the Japanese room. The self-portrait (433) is even more interesting. On this wall are pictures that offer a striking comparison of methods of painting.

Gallery 3 is made especially interesting by the domination of one man, Maurice Denis, who is the leader among the "advanced" decorators of France. There is much that is worthy of study in the simplicity and in the color of his panels here. The room contains also a number of examples of the new and ultra-new schools, from Monet and Degas to Redon and Puy.

Gallery 4 contains few outstanding features, the more conservative element predominating. There is charming color in Caro-Delvaille's canvas on the East wall (279), and there is a Lucien Simon on the south wall. Gallery 5 likewise is not very important.

Gallery 6 especially illustrates the decorative tendency. On the north wall are panels by Auburtin, a follower of de Chavannes, and by Devoux, which are pure decorations. On the south wall is a large canvas by the celebrated Menard; but his little seascape on the west wall (445) is more appealing, being one of the most attractive things in the section. Note how the decorative tendency characterizes not only these outdoor pictures, but the neighboring portraits as well. On the east wall is a canvas by le Sidaner, a leader of the plein-air school, which reminds one that good French landscapes are few in this exhibit.

The Italian Section is the best arranged in the galleries. There is a general feeling of orderliness and rest that is quite welcome as one comes from the overcrowded American rooms. The Italian paintings do not give the impression of an exhibition of masterpieces-indeed there are very few canvases that demand special notice-but they are well up to the average set in the other sections.

Gallery 21 is the most interesting. On the wall facing the main doorway are five pictures by Ettore Tito, perhaps the greatest and certainly the most popular, of Italian painters. All are strong, and they are painted with a bigness and a sureness of touch that are compelling. Very interesting too are the canvases on the adjoining wall by Camillo Innocenti, who has achieved the vibrating light and fresh coloring of the Impressionist School in an individual way.

Gallery 22 contains a varied collection, ranging from the academic to the radical. Here are two canvases by Arturo Noci, one of the leaders of the Italian Secession. Gallery 23 is given up mainly to sculpture. The most compelling thing is d'Orsi's realistic "Tired Peasant." With the exception of some of the small bronzes, the rest of the sculpture of the section is hardly notable.

Gallery 24 contains a very interesting canvas in Plinio Nomellini's picture of a woman and child in a boat drawn up under a tree. The thing is full of sunlight and sparkling color; and it strikes a good medium between the old tight painting and that which carries Impressionism too far-both of which extremes can be seen in plenty in this room. Gallery 25 is an average room, without special features.

The Cuban Section occupies gallery 20, next to the Italian section. There is hardly a picture here that does not seem labored in comparison with the freedom elsewhere.

The Uruguay Section, in the adjoining gallery 19, is just the opposite full of freshness and vigor, and brilliant in color. But the gift of brilliancy is rather undisciplined, and while there is unmistakable promise, one feels that the art of Uruguay has not yet found itself.

The Chinese Section occupies galleries 94 to 97, and is notable for the paintings on silk and paper, the cloisonne, and the lacquer. There is a wealth of interesting material in the display, but it really requires a great amount of study for full appreciation. The Chinese Commission has prepared a special catalogue, which can be had in the rooms if one is specially interested.

The Philippine Section, in the adjoining gallery 98, is almost negligible in a building where there is so much really worth seeing though some of the paintings by Felix Hidalgo have a dramatic interest.

The Swedish Section, in galleries 99 to 107, is one of the most important in the building. One who likes a gentle, polished sort of art will not be at home here; but for virile, fresh and colorful painting there is no other section that achieves the same high standard. Many of the pictures are so strong and big that they never should have been put in these box-like little rooms, where a proper perspective is impossible. In the paintings there are traces of French and German training, and especially of Impressionism; but the exhibit shows more true national feeling and more individual independence than any other in the building.

The two featured groups are the remarkable paintings and tapestries of Gustav Adolf Fjaestad in gallery 107-well worthy of long study-and the paintings and prints of Carl Larsson in gallery 101. But there are many other things quite as important: the brilliant and fresh canvases of Carlburg, the snow scenes touched with late sunlight, by Schultzberg, and the compelling autumn decorations by Osslund, all in gallery 102; the illustrations by Bauer in gallery 104; the big landscapes by Hesselborn in gallery 105; and the deep-toned studies by Anna Boberg, and the virile portraits, in gallery 106. If you doubt that these Swedish painters can do the polished, poetic thing, as well as the big vigorous sort, go back to gallery 103, and look at Bergstrom's atmospheric "Spring Day."

The Swedish sculpture is not so remarkable as the painting; but the print section in gallery 99 contains a number of very interesting etchings and wood engravings.

The Argentine Section, in gallery 112, shows much that is fresh, strong, and brilliant in color. It is interesting to see how much closer these South American painters are to Spain than to France and Germany. Here are many echoes, not only of Velasquez and Goya, but of the vital modern Spaniards like Zuloaga. The collection is very uneven; but in the work of men like Jorge Bermudez and Hector Nava there is a mighty promise if not any great achievement. The few sculptures are unusually strong and interesting.

The Portuguese Section, in galleries 109 to 111, has the appearance of belonging to an older period in the history of art than the present. One feels that the artists who show pictures here have not that mastery of light which marks the Nineteenth Century's greatest advance in painting. Certainly there is evidence of a general reliance on the older standards. Perhaps the best works are those of Columbano, in the central gallery. Here too, and in the next room, are some realistic works of Malhoa that compel attention.

The International Room, gallery 108, contains all that the Exposition has of German work. On wall C are such splendid things as Leo Putz' "The Shore" and Heinrich von Zugel's "In the Rhine Meadows;" and on wall A is Franz Stuck's "Summer Night"-by no means one of this decorator's best works, though characteristically rich and deep-toned. But one feels the lack of those others who have lately lifted Germany back among the greatest nations artistically: von Uhde, Liebermann, von Gebhardt, Klinger, Erler, and von Hofmann. In the same way the young and virile English group is not represented, though in this room is a passable portrait by the great John Lavery. On wall D are two Spanish works of Lopez-Mezquita, that are worthy of attention but nothing of Zuloaga or Sorolla.

The Holland Section, occupying galleries 113-116, contains a display that is well balanced but without outstanding features. There are echoes of many departed glories, of Rembrandt, of Hals, and even of the French Barbizon men, and a few typical beautifully lighted Dutch interiors. But there is none of the work of the men whom the art magazines have taught us to consider the representative Dutch painters of today: Israels, the Maris brothers, and Mauve. The print room is likewise good rather than splendid, unless one excepts M. A. J. Bauer's fine Rembrandtian etchings. Charles van Wyck's small bronzes are notable among the sculptures.

Scattered Art Exhibits State and Foreign Buildings

The Palace of Fine Arts has been reserved exclusively for painting, sculpture and prints, with the result that the material of the usual "arts and crafts" exhibitions has been badly scattered. Certain exhibits have been taken to the state and foreign buildings, some of which are also of interest architecturally; but most of the craftswork is to be found in the four exhibition palaces on the Avenue of Palms.

The Palace of Varied Industries contains, between 5th and 6th Streets, three important displays: at Avenue A is Denmark's exhibition of porcelain and pottery, with a small section devoted to the book arts; at Avenue B is an excellent display of German porcelain; and at Avenue D is the Netherlands exhibit of porcelain and pottery. At 4th Street and Avenue C is the exhibition of Chinese arts and crafts. The American section of so-called "Domestic Arts and Crafts" is at 1st Street and Avenue C, and contains a very small but select showing of all the usual handicrafts. Elsewhere in the building there are minor displays of textiles, ceramics, tapestries, silver work, and interior decoration, installed by commercial firms. One can see looms working, jewelry being made, and China being painted.

The Palace of Manufactures is notable for the extensive arts and crafts exhibit of Japan, which covers almost one-quarter of the building's floor space; for that of Italy, which includes a large number of statuettes besides the usual departments; and for those of France, and Great Britain and Ireland. One will find all of these displays by walking along Avenue C.

The Palace of Liberal Arts contains a few exhibits of the book arts and architecture. The most important architectural display is that in the United States Government Section, shown by the National Fine Arts Commission. On Avenue D between 1st and 5th Streets there are displays of fine photography.

The Palace of Education contains the exhibition of the American art schools, at Avenue B and 6th Street. At Avenue E and 3rd Street pottery is made.

In the group of palaces on the Marina there is little to interest in art matters. In the Mines Palace the Government's exhibit of coins and medals is of some interest. In the Transportation Palace the student of applied art can find much to think about in the relation of art to automobile design. In the Agriculture and Food Products Palaces there is little to attract the art-lover except at meal-time.

The Italian Buildings contain an extensive museum of national historic art and archaeology, which is well worth seeing. The mural painting in the Royal Salon represents "The Glorification of Italy." The buildings reproduce historic Italian styles of architecture. The charming central court, the gardens, and the buildings contain many replicas of masterpieces of sculpture.

The French Building was unfinished at the time this was written (June first), but it is to contain an extensive art display. There are to be a number of statues by Rodin, the greatest of modern sculptors, which alone would make a visit imperative for every art lover.

The Swedish Building is one of the most interesting architecturally, suggesting the fine originality of recent Scandinavian architecture. It is worthy of note too, that the Norwegian and Danish buildings strike a note of freshness that is in fine contrast with most of the foreign pavilions. In all three of these buildings there are small exhibits of painting and handiwork.

The Turkish Building contains an attractive exhibit of rugs; and in the
Philippine Building there is a display of metal work and basketry.

The State Buildings are in general designed for social purposes. That of Pennsylvania is an interesting bit of Colonial architecture, and contains two virile and colorful decorations by John Trumbull, representing "Penn's Treaty with the Indians" and "The Industries of Pennsylvania." The Maryland Building is also a simple, dignified bit of Colonial design. The Massachusetts Building reproduces the famous "Bulfinch front" of the Boston State House. The Mission style of architecture is pleasingly exemplified in the California Building.